CONCEPTUAL FOUNDATIONS OF SOCIAL RESEARCH METHODS

Randall Koetting
Spring 2007

CONCEPTUAL FOUNDATIONS OF SOCIAL RESEARCH METHODS

DAVID BARONOV

Paradigm Publishers

BOULDER • LONDON

Copyright © 2004 by Paradigm Publishers

Published in the United States by Paradigm Publishers, 3360 Mitchell Lane, Suite E, Boulder, Colorado 80301 USA.

Paradigm Publishers is the trade name of Birkenkamp & Company, LLC, Dean Birkenkamp, President and Publisher.

Library of Congress Cataloging-in-Publication Data

Baronov, David.
Conceptual foundations of social research methods / David Baronov.
p. cm.
Includes index.
ISBN 1-59451-070-9 (cloth : alk. paper) — ISBN 1-59451-071-7 (pbk : alk. paper)
ISBN 13: 978-1-59451-070-0 (cloth)—ISBN 13: 978-1-59451-071-7 (pbk)
1. Social sciences—Research—Methodology. 2. Social sciences—Research—Philosophy. I. Title.

H62.B337 2004
300'.72—dc22   2004006927

Printed and bound in the United States of America on acid-free paper that meets the standards of the American National Standard for Permanence of Paper for Printed Library Materials.

Designed and Typeset by Straight Creek Bookmakers.

10   09   08   07
5   4   3   2

Contents

Acknowledgments

I owe a great debt to many students, friends, and colleagues whose insights and inspiration have shaped my understanding of the core issues explored in this book. Terence Hopkins, Dale Tomich, and Kelvin Santiago Valles were among those who first encouraged me to pursue the disturbing entanglements beneath the surface of methodological issues in the social sciences. Their advice, suggestions, and criticisms continue to prod my interest in the field. Good fortune has allowed me to further consider the implications of these issues through conversations and exchanges with a number of talented colleagues, including Erik Pérez Velasco, Gladys Jiménez Muñoz, Ruth L. Harris, Robert Brimlow, José Toro Alfonso, Khaldoun Samman, and Mark Gaskill.

I am especially grateful for the contributions of Timothy Madigan and Daniel R. Shaffer, whose reviews and comments on earlier drafts of the manuscript were critical for the development of this work. I have also greatly benefited from the skillful assistance of my publisher, Dean Birkenkamp. His encouragement was essential for seeing this project through to its completion and guiding me along the path.

In 2002, I was the recipient of a St. John Fisher College Faculty Development Grant. This award provided me with critical resources and financial assistance for the completion of this project.

Lastly, I wish to acknowledge the essential contribution of Mrs. Druian, without whom this book would never have been possible.

Introduction and Fair Warning

By now the routine is a familiar one. Each fall, anxious throngs of high school graduates—and a growing number of adult returning students—make their way onto college campuses. The new arrivals face the formidable tasks of working toward graduation and preparing for a career. This requires, early on, selecting a major. The major will clarify graduation requirements and provide a sense of career options. Ominously, the selection of a major will also lock unsuspecting students into a mind-set and a framework of analysis that will tell them, quite literally, what and how to think, the nature of truth, and which questions are permitted and which are not.

Traditionally, college subjects are grouped into three branches—humanities, physical sciences, and social sciences. Each encompasses a distinct subject matter and each explores this subject matter through a unique battery of methods. The humanities study forms of creative human expression (art, literature, music, etc.) and deploy various interpretive methods. The physical sciences study the natural world and rely upon the so-called scientific method. The social sciences study the social world (forms of human interaction and individual behavior) and turn to variations of the scientific method. Curiously, in the course of one's undergraduate education, while there is a good deal of recognition and discussion about the distinct subject matters that separate the three branches, little is said of the differences between the branches' methods.

The consequences of this oversight can be insidious. Consider the experiences of Fawziyya, Lisa, and Manuel—three seventeen-year-olds who were among those arriving on campus last fall. As it happened, all had suffered the painful loss of their mother to cancer in the past year. All three were, of course, deeply affected by their mothers' deaths and these personal tragedies dramatically shaped how they chose a college major. Fawziyya wanted to understand the nature of her mother's illness so she could help others. She chose to study biology. Lisa was curious why, despite

1

the dangers, certain cancer-related practices (such as smoking) are so prevalent across society. She chose to study sociology. Manuel wanted to better appreciate the spiritual and emotional transformation that his mother experienced while dying of cancer. He chose to study literature. Each struggled to come to terms with a deeply personal loss and each chose a separate path. In the end, a common tragedy—a mother's death from cancer—resulted in three distinct forms of knowledge and insight.

Directly tied to these distinct forms of knowledge and insight are methods of analysis that determine how one sees and understands the world. These are the implicit anchors (and the ideology) defining the boundaries of any field. For this reason, they are crucial and, for this reason, they are dangerous. In light of this, a rather absurd situation prevails today. In the course of an undergraduate education, each student confronts a set of fundamental assumptions and presuppositions concerning the nature of truth attached to his or her field of study. However, with rare exception, there is little sustained discussion of these assumptions and presuppositions in comparison with other fields. As a result, students pursue truth within the confines of their field and become the unwitting transmitters of its silent ideology. The purpose of this book is to explicitly address the unexplored assumptions and hidden ideologies that lurk beneath a college education. While there is a particular focus on the social sciences (in particular sociology), there is also much to be gained by those in the humanities and the physical sciences who wish to better understand the role of unspoken premises within their own fields.

SOME BASIC ISSUES

The search for truth shapes all fields of inquiry. Within the social sciences, the notion of truth and the methods used to uncover it have for centuries undergone—and continue to undergo—constant reflection and revision. How best to investigate the social world remains an open question. However, the debates concerning scientific inquiry in the social sciences have evolved along a discernible path with certain recurring issues and themes. The purpose in considering these debates is not to discover the one unassailable method but to better appreciate the plurality of competing method-ological traditions that inform contemporary scientific inquiry in the social sciences. Four recurrent issues in particular tend to frame issues and shape this debate. These include the legacy of positiv-ism, the link between the social sciences and the physical sciences, the nature of facts versus values, and the roles of rationalism and empiricism.

The development of scientific inquiry within the social sciences has largely been the product of the European Enlightenment and its contested legacy of positivism. It would be difficult to exagger-ate the enduring influence of the Enlightenment on contemporary discussions of scientific inquiry. The era of the Enlightenment was a protracted period of radical questioning. The professed purpose of such questioning was the search for truth. All claims of truth were subject to intense scrutiny. The reliance on tradition was thrown out as mere superstition. The authority of the church was no longer recognized. The subjective claims of metaphysics were rejected. To replace all these, an objective method of scientific inquiry was established. This method quickly gained favor among those investigating the world of nature. When those investigating the social world likewise adopted this approach, they referred to their method of scientific inquiry as positivism. The positivists en-deavored to erase all subjective bias from the study of society. Neither the researcher's views nor those of the human subjects could be allowed to influence the results. The legacy of these early efforts to minimize subjectivity within scientific inquiry in the social sciences remains with us to this day.

Based on these early developments, serious reservations soon surfaced regarding the social sciences' reliance on a model of investigation derived from the physical sciences. The first concert-ed efforts to establish the social sciences as a distinct and coherent field began in the nineteenth century. At the time, the physical sciences already enjoyed an enviable reputation among leading European intellectuals. This followed from the impressive advances of the physical sciences in the seventeenth and eighteenth centu-ries in the areas of astronomy and physics. Given the demonstrable progress of the physical sciences in the production of knowledge, most people simply assumed that the natural course of develop-ment for the less mature social sciences would be to follow the example of the physical sciences. From their birth, therefore, the agenda and orientation of the social sciences were married to those of the physical sciences. The benefits and the limitations of this fateful matrimony have served as a source of both boastful pride and emphatic dissent ever since.

A further issue shaping scientific inquiry in the social sciences takes the form of a conflict between facts and values. This conflict grows directly from the debate concerning the influence of the physical sciences. In short, it is argued that the nature of the subject matter investigated by the physical sciences differs significantly from that of the social sciences. The physical sciences concern themselves with facts (value-neutral objects such as a rock, an atom, or a star). The social sciences concern themselves with values (value-laden objects such as a prisoner, a patient, or a single mother). The principal difference between a value-neutral object and a value-laden object is the need, in the case of the latter, to account for its social meaning. For example, what it means to be a prisoner is shaped by social norms and beliefs, while the analysis of the organic composition of a rock raises no such concerns. At issue, therefore, is whether these differences in subject matter are reconcilable within the model of scientific inquiry borrowed from the physical sciences. Many doubt this. As a result, it has been argued that there are lingering contradictions and internal inconsistencies within the social sciences that prevent them from fully understanding their subject matter on the basis of the continuing influence of the physical sciences.

Lastly, there remains the perennial struggle between advocates of rationalism and advocates of empiricism regarding the proper foundation for truth. This issue first surfaced among researchers in the physical sciences and its consequences are no less relevant for the social sciences. In essence, it is argued that there are two principal bases for establishing truth. On one side, advocates of rationalism emphasize the role of logical deduction. They contend that absolute certainty can only be the product of a structured, logical argument in which certain conclusions necessarily follow from an established set of premises. On the other side, advocates of empiricism emphasize the role of direct observation and experience. They argue that absolute certainty can only be the product of immediate sense data. In truth, few zealots would consider abandoning empiricism in the pursuit of pure rationalism or vice versa. However, the simmering tension between these two sources of knowledge provides a common backdrop for all of the approaches to scientific inquiry within the social sciences.

A unique feature of the debate concerning scientific inquiry in the social sciences is the fact that one does not have the option to remain neutral. In the very act of carrying out scientific inquiry one is implicated. This is true whether a researcher's intentions are explicitly stated or merely implicitly present in the course of investigation. A potential peril emerges from this that demands due warning. While one must adopt a method of scientific inquiry—and all the assumptions and presuppositions that go with it—one is not necessarily required to analyze the consequences of this choice. Herein lies the danger. Across the social sciences, much scientific inquiry proceeds with the naïve researcher oblivious to its built-in assumptions and hidden agendas. For a researcher, questioning one's own fundamental assumptions regarding the nature of truth can be, to say the least, unsettling. Beyond this, however, it can provoke the wrath of those researchers (and instructors in research methods courses) who prefer to live happily with the illusion of unexamined certainty and who therefore have little tolerance for those who countenance such subversive thoughts.

BASIC TOPICS

This book is organized into seven chapters. Each of the first six chapters provides an overview of a specific approach to scientific inquiry in the social sciences. Given the disproportionate impact of positivism on the modern social sciences, the first half of the book is dedicated to discussing its basic features and historical evolution. The first three chapters concern various stages in the maturation of positivism: nineteenth-century embryonic positivism, early-twentieth-century logical positivism, and present-day postpositivism. Chapter 4 addresses the unique contributions of structuralism as a form of scientific inquiry. Chapter 5 details the withering assault of hermeneutics on the fundamental premises of positivism and its rejection of subjectivity. Chapter 6 reviews the relentless antifoundationalist attacks on reason itself as an adequate criterion of truth. Chapter 7 explores the practical and ethical consequences of the methodological choices that confront social researchers through the example of a common undergraduate research project.

Embryonic positivism refers to the initial period of positivism's development. At this stage, the advocates of embryonic positivism were primarily preoccupied with translating the categories and techniques of analysis from the physical sciences into a language for the social sciences. The rudimentary forms of observation and experimentation in the social world, along with rules for deductive and inductive reasoning, were formalized. The proponents of embryonic positivism took it upon themselves to convince a skeptical public that phenomena in the social world were as amenable to formalized scientific inquiry as were phenomena in the natural world. The table of contents of any standard social research methods textbook in the twenty-first century provides convincing evidence of their remarkable success.

Logical positivism represented an effort to narrow the scope of embryonic positivism and to refine its manner of investigation. The primary concern of logical positivism was the construction of a precise language of observation and explanation for the social world. It became imperative that this language add nothing beyond that which was literally observed. In essence, the proponents of logical positivism sought to re-create the social world through a type of language that was free of observer bias and that could logically link pure observation statements in a causal chain to other such statements. The ultimate goal was to provide logically sound explanations of social phenomena based on empirical observation. This required an understanding of the manner by which scientific inquiry moved from observation to description and from description to explanation that went well beyond that of embryonic positivism.

Postpositivism was, in part, a reaction to the narrowing definitions of scientific inquiry and a certain confusion concerning the investigation of the social world that had developed under logical positivism. Proponents of postpositivism argue that the standard of absolute certainty for knowledge is not realistic. This argument signaled the move from a social science based on absolute truth to one based on degrees of probability. Furthermore, proponents of postpositivism suggest that greater attention must be paid to the difficulty of making pure, untainted observations. All observations will, in fact, to some degree be influenced by the perspective directing the investigation. In this sense, all observations are theory laden. Proponents of postpositivism argue that the loss of absolute certainty and the problem of theory-laden observations are by no means reasons for giving up scientific inquiry. They are merely limitations that must be taken into account when investigating the social world.

Structuralism emerged as a strategy to thwart the tendency of many positivists to treat social phenomena as isolated and discrete entities. Structuralists rejected the notion of reducing social phenomena to their most basic and elementary form as a means to understand them. Rather, they argued that all social phenomena were defined not by properties specific to an entity but by the social context in which one found the entity. This required a major transformation in how one interpreted social phenomena. Direct observation and measurement were no longer sufficient. Structuralists argued that to understand social phenomena required dissecting the social conditions that gave rise to and sustained an entity. The social conditions were as important as—if not more important than—the social fact.

Hermeneutics provided an early critique of positivism based on alleged differences between the subject matter of the social sciences and that of the physical sciences. Positivism, it was believed, was the appropriate perspective of the latter but not the former. Proponents of hermeneutics insisted that the nature of social phenomena required an analysis of the meaning behind human thought and action. Owing to positivism's strict value-neutral approach, it could not grasp the true meaning of value-laden social phenomena. Instead, proponents of hermeneutics called for investigative techniques that could recover the subjective meaning behind human action and social development.

Antifoundationalism provides a critical return to scientific inquiry's Enlightenment roots and, in a most disturbing manner, it proceeds to raise fundamental questions about the ability of human reason to produce reliable knowledge about the social world. The legitimacy of the Enlightenment's most basic project—the search for truth—is itself open to critique. Proponents of antifoundationalism suggest that the legacy of positivism (and of structuralism) has inspired heroic efforts to bring order and stability to a fragmented and chaotic social world. The result is an exercise in distortion and ideology that—rather than reveal the social world as it truly is— merely reveals established patterns of social power. Ultimately, the descriptions and prescriptions of the social sciences reflect the dominant social order. The search for truth is illusory.

A few caveats are in order. The first concerns a basic limitation. The manner by which methodological issues are considered here is decidedly Eurocentric. Space does not allow a full consideration of the contributions outside of Western European traditions. The attempts by social researchers in Africa and Latin America, for example, to reframe methodological issues to fit their unique sociohistorical settings have resulted in much innovative thinking in the past few decades. Nonetheless, those interested in pursuing these developments outside of Western European traditions will still find this book a useful resource insofar as—owing to centuries of colonial rule—most of the alternative approaches continue to frame their ideas in reference to (or juxtaposition with) Western European traditions.

The second caveat concerns the nature of contributions to certain traditions. Importantly, the material presented here has been organized, not to faithfully replicate the actual historical debates, but to highlight major issues and debates over time. Discussions and debates are organized around what, in hindsight, constitute key contributions irrespective of the precise historical chronology. For example, chapter 3 refers to a group called the "late logical positivists." In the chapter, they are treated as a coherent cohort although, in fact, the works cited span four decades and some members never directly engaged one another. Furthermore, some contributors to a debate occasionally contest their affiliation with a certain tradition. Both Ernst Mach (1838–1916) and Bertrand Russell (1872–1970) famously rejected the positivist label. Nonetheless, each is considered a significant contributor to the positivist tradition. Thus, for the sake of highlighting tendencies within a particular methodological approach, it is helpful to organize major works according to themes rather than always following the strict historical order or a given contributor's personal preferences.

Finally, one might note that the aim of this text is both modest and ambitious. The modest aim is to provide the reader with a basic introduction to the issues and debates beneath the surface of social research methods and to highlight key contributions. Somewhat more ambitiously, the following chapters survey a wide range of subjects and topics whose nuances and complexities arguably defy the format of an introductory overview. Indeed, many of the topics treated here have elsewhere received voluminous attention in the specialized literature. Literally hundreds of scholarly texts are available, for example, that address the thought of Francis Bacon or Auguste Comte as subjects of studies unto themselves. The same is true for the Vienna Circle or structuralism. The role of a work such as this is, therefore, very specific. It is to introduce the uninitiated reader to a series of issues and debates in the social sciences in a manner that is both economical and intentional. A fuller consideration of these matters is available to readers through the suggested readings at the end of each chapter and the primary sources identified throughout the text.

FURTHER READING

Hollis, Martin. "Introduction: Problems of Structure and Action." Pp. 1–22 in *The Philosophy of Social Science*. New York: Cambridge University Press, 1994.

Jarvie, I. C. "Philosophy of the Social Sciences." Pp. 604–8 in *The Social Science Encyclopedia*, 2nd ed. Edited by Adam Kuper and Jessica Kuper. New York: Routledge, 1996.

MacIntyre, Alasdair. "The Idea of a Social Science." Pp. 15–33 in *The Philosophy of Social Explanation*. Edited by Alan Ryan. London: Oxford University Press, 1973.

Taylor, Charles. "Interpretation and the Sciences of Man." Pp. 15–58 in *Philosophy and the Human Sciences: Philosophical Papers 2*. New York: Cambridge University Press, 1985.

1

Embryonic Positivism

What Is Embryonic Positivism?

The strengthening birth pangs of nineteenth-century positivism signaled the first systematic effort to adapt those research methods originally developed for the physical sciences to the study of society. While conceding certain basic differences, the excited enthusiasts of the emerging positivist era were adamant that the methods perfected for the study of the physical world provided equally powerful tools for the study of the social world. The rationale for this was straightforward. The most advanced and sophisticated research methods of the day had been developed and had proven their worth in the physical sciences. It was therefore only logical that the study of human society should begin with the most potent techniques of investigation available.

What followed was a mad rush to apply the standards of investigation of the physical sciences to the social world. It was hoped, and wholly expected, that in short order all social phenomena would be explained and reduced to a single, uniform set of general laws—just as Newton's three laws of motion had been applied to the physical world. While many attempts ended in folly, it can certainly be argued that these early architects of the social world remain the primary influence upon those who study society today. At the apex of such efforts was a slightly self-absorbed French intellectual. Auguste Comte's (1798–1857) public career may have ended with the rejection of his generous offer to serve as the high priest of his newly devised universal religion unifying all of humanity. However, while most were as yet unprepared to trust their soul to Comte, many took heed of his insightful descriptions of society and the novel methods he devised for its investigation. This was the origin of embryonic positivism.

Embryonic positivism represented an early stage in the development of a distinct approach to understanding society. The specific methods of investigation included empirical observation, comparisons of conditions, and experimental verification of hypotheses and theories. It was hoped that through careful, systematic observation, comparison, and experimentation certain general laws about society would be uncovered. Owing to the undeveloped nature of embryonic positivism, the primary emphasis was on empirical observation and the nature of what one could properly conclude from it. In particular, the promoters of embryonic positivism struggled to remove all remnants of metaphysical reasoning. Metaphysics referred to systems of knowledge that relied upon assumptions about the world that were not immediately observable. For example, for embryonic positivism, the claim that the world had been created by God amounted to a fanciful fiction and, while it gave comfort to its inventors, such reasoning was without empirical foundation and unworthy of scientific consideration.

The broad and lasting influence of Comte and others in this regard is undeniable. Herbert Spencer (1820–1903) in England, Emile Durkheim (1858–1917) in France, and Ferdinand Tönnies (1855–1936) in Germany, among other luminaries of social thought, drew direct inspiration from these works. However, as will be seen later in this book, by the close of the early twentieth century, Comte's grand vision of positivism came to be regarded more as a mere passing, adolescent phase.

WHAT ARE THE ORIGINS OF EMBRYONIC POSITIVISM?

The seeds of embryonic positivism were first sown in the late sixteenth and seventeenth centuries. Its story marries two traditions: British empiricism and the scientific revolution. British empiricism is a broad and complex philosophical tradition that survives to this day. The basic tenets of empiricism revolve around the nature of how one makes observations and how one experiences and understands the world. Its advocates argue that all one can know about the world is limited to that which we experience through our five senses. Empiricists begin by formulating statements that describe these observations or experiences. However, there is a great deal of controversy surrounding just how one moves from descriptions of the world based on our five senses to explanations of the world based on our powers of reasoning and conjecture. The inductive method was developed by empiricists to move from observation to explanation and, within embryonic positivism, this was a central tool of investigation.

The extraordinary discoveries and breakthroughs of the scientific revolution opened people's eyes to new understandings of the physical world. The remarkable tools for these discoveries—though at the time still evolving—were referred to in shorthand as the scientific method; this was believed to be the surest path to a true understanding of the world as it actually functioned. Most importantly, the startling claims and revolutionary insights derived from this new scientific method could be demonstrated. The claims of science were not mere pronouncements but resulted in concrete and practical innovations that people could see and that ultimately came to reshape their daily lives.

Bacon, Hume, and British Empiricism

Francis Bacon (1561–1626) was among the earliest thinkers in a long line of British empiricists. He made three principal contributions to embryonic positivism. First, Bacon carried on an unrestrained and devastating critique of the Aristotelian scientific tradition then in vogue. Second, he insisted on judging the value of all new knowledge, ultimately, by the criterion of its social utility—its ability to directly advance technological progress. Third, in dismissing the Aristotelian deductive method as hopelessly empty, Bacon promoted an alternative inductive method as the best means available for making new discoveries about the world.

Above all, he sought to finally and definitively supplant the Aristotelian tradition of deductive reasoning as the standard method of scientific investigation. The deductive method consisted of first stating a claim and then logically deducing statements that would follow from this. This took the popular form of a syllogism—a type of argument based upon a major premise, a minor premise, and a conclusion that follows therefrom. A common syllogism at the time was: All men are mortal. Socrates is a man. Therefore, Socrates is mortal. This may be true, Bacon and others assuredly agreed. However, it was truth at the expense of knowledge. Deduction added nothing new to our original base of knowledge. The purpose of science, Bacon maintained, was not simply to derive simple truths from basic logic but to make new discoveries about the world.

Bacon published *Novum Organum* in 1620. This can be roughly rendered "New Methodology of Science" and was explicitly written to replace Aristotle's *Organum*. Like an idol, Bacon argued, the old science had no substance and survived as a mere image, unworthy of worship. Bacon's dismissal of Aristotelian science as a form of idol worship was critical insofar as it represented a definitive historical turning point in which the physical sciences made a break from previous, long-revered methods of investigation.

Bacon launched his vitriolic attack against idol worship on four fronts: the Idols of the Tribe, the Idols of the Cave, the Idols of the Marketplace, and the Idols of the Theatre. The Idols of the Tribe concerned the deceptive role of wishful thinking. Bacon argued that there was a general human tendency to overvalue that which agrees with one's preconceptions and to overlook that which disagrees. To the extent that this was allowed to interfere with scientific inquiry one was easily led astray. The Idols of the Cave pointed to the subjective nature of individual understanding and how this distorted scientific thinking. Bacon argued that one of the principal challenges of science was to develop a method of inquiry that allowed scientific knowledge to grow beyond a random collection of individual beliefs and to create a common base of knowledge. The influence of individual bias and prejudice had to be somehow filtered out so that all fair-minded persons would reach the same conclusion when confronted with similar facts.

The Idols of the Marketplace critiqued the imprecise and ambiguous use of language. In describing physical properties, Bacon maintained, it was important to move beyond words that convey a general sense (such as heavy or light) and move to a more exact language (such as forty pounds or ten pounds). He was one of the first in a long line of modern scientific thinkers to yearn for a precise language for science. The Idols of the Theatre took on the predominant philosophical systems of the day, such as Aristotelianism and Scholasticism. Here, Bacon's critique was without mercy. These were the principal influences that shaped people's worldviews; they precluded the discovery of the world as it truly was because they claimed to already know its true nature. In their place, Bacon sought to advance systematic observation, comparison, and experimentation.

Bacon was convinced that the true purpose of science was social progress and technological utility. He was particularly upset with those who toiled in the Aristotelian tradition because they had made little if any contribution to the technological advances that marked important developments in society (such as printing, gunpowder, or the magnet). The measure of true science, according to Bacon, was its ability to yield further inventions for society. This was the marriage of empiricism and reason. Empiricism provided a window into the world, while reason allowed one to organize knowledge of this world, thus leading to progress.

The role of reason was to provide insight into abstract relationships on the basis of empirical observations. If these abstract relationships were general truths, then they would yield information beyond the empirical observations and lead to the prediction of future observations. From this follows Bacon's oft repeated maxim, Knowledge is power. In a clever analogy, Bacon likened the purely rationalist approach to that of a spider who weaves a web from a substance of its own creation. The empiricist who operates without rationality was compared to the ant that gathers and uses materials with little sense of how to organize and sort them. The empiricist who deftly combines observations with rationality was likened to the bee that gathers and digests material, adding its own substance and creating a new product of higher value.

Bacon's importance as an inspiration for embryonic positivism followed largely from his critique of the emptiness of science linked to the dominant Aristotelian tradition and his insistence that true science must lead to technological progress and social utility. In addition, Bacon introduced and further developed a highly influential method of scientific investigation, the inductive method—one of his principal contributions to the history of science. This followed from his critique of the deductive method. If the deductive method did not lead to the development of new knowledge, Bacon concluded, it could not be the basis for science. The inductive method was, therefore, required. Importantly, the deductive method was by no means simply discarded. In fact, it came to represent the essential rationalist component that allowed one to derive general truths from individual observations.

Bacon's basic insight was that deductive logic alone was not sufficient to move from observed facts to general truths and specific predictions about future observations. He discarded Aristotle's empty syllogism that ends with the notion that "Socrates is mortal." In its place, he constructed inferential statements. In inferential statements, the conclusion is not *necessarily* contained in the statement. An inferential statement takes past observations and extends them to future observations. The conclusion is not guaranteed. For example: All frogs observed thus far have been green. Therefore, all frogs are green. In this case the conclusion (all frogs are green) is not guaranteed by the premise (all frogs observed thus far have been green). The conclusion that "all frogs are green" is an inductive inference and can only be verified or falsified by future observation. The use of the inductive method was a shattering break from the original standard of absolute, certain knowledge based on mathematical precision as established by the Greeks and marked a new era of scientific inquiry.

The person to most fully develop the inductive method (and its internal contradictions) was another British empiricist, David Hume (1711–1776), laboring in Bacon's long shadow. Hume's principal contribution to the development of embryonic positivism was his unsettling critique of pure empiricism as a standard of absolute, certain knowledge. This argument was most fully developed in one of the most influential works of the age, *Enquiries Concerning Human Understanding,* published by Hume in 1748. Hume began with the simple claim that the only basis for any knowledge was either rationalism (analytical knowledge) or empiricism (empirical knowledge).

Analytical knowledge was based on deduction. Empirical knowledge relied upon the inductive method, as developed by Bacon. Hume observed that a unique feature of the inductive method—not true for the deductive method—was that one could imagine a conclusion to be false while the premise remained true. Returning to the previous example, it was argued that because all previously observed frogs were green, we could expect that all future frogs would likewise be green. However, logically speaking, it was possible to imagine that the conclusion was false (that, in fact, a future frog would not be green) while the premise (that all previously observed frogs had been green) remained true. Hume concluded from this that the inductive method did not imply logical necessity, as did rationalism and the deductive method.

Hume, in fact, had uncovered a rather troubling circular logic within the inductive method. One believed in induction simply because induction had worked in the past. (We believe that all future frogs will be green because all past frogs have been green.) This led to Hume's second troubling conclusion. The truth of conclusions based on the inductive method cannot be accepted with absolute certainty. Therefore, any inferences based on the inductive method are suspect. A fundamental dilemma arose for empiricists and presented two options. The first option was to become a pure empiricist and admit no statements unless they were either (a) rationalist in nature (based on deduction) or (b) derived directly from observation and experience. As a result, the pure empiricist would have to forfeit the ability to predict future events. Rationalism was based on a deductive method that yielded no new knowledge (and therefore foretold no future happenings) while strict observation led only to baseless speculation about yet-to-occur events.

The second option was to simply proceed with the inductive method while freely admitting that the inferences drawn therefrom—those not immediately based on observation and experience—were not empirical. One had abandoned pure empiricism as a standard of truth. The predominant belief of Hume's age held that true knowledge—knowledge contributing to a greater understanding of the world—must produce reliable predictions about events in the world or it was useless. Hume demonstrated that pure empiricism cannot yield true knowledge; therefore, with Hume, empiricism entered into a period of deep crisis. As the definitive statement on the limitations of the inductive method, Hume's work pointed to the emerging recognition that a new standard of knowledge was required for modern science.

Galileo, Newton, and the Scientific Revolution

The scientific revolution was notable for more than the new scientific facts that were added to the store of human knowledge (such as Galileo's uniform rates of falling bodies or Newton's three laws of motion). Such discoveries, admittedly, were astounding and advanced humankind's understanding exponentially. However, equally remarkable was the particular manner by which such discoveries were made. Galileo, Newton, and others had not merely stumbled upon novel descriptions of the physical world. They had created a method of discovery that would serve as a blueprint for the physical sciences for generations to come.

In this regard, it is helpful to organize discussion around the works of two of the greatest contributors to the scientific revolution, Galileo Galilei (1564–1642) and Isaac Newton (1642–1727). In the case of Galileo, his influence encompassed several areas: (1) his insistence upon the need for experimental confirmation, (2) his development of the hypothetico-deductive method, and (3) his rejection of teleological explanations. Newton's impact on the scientific method, no less dramatic than Galileo's, revolved around his efforts (1) to foster further advances in experimental confirmation and (2) to develop the hypothetico-deductive method in greater detail.

Galileo completed *The Dialogue Concerning Two Chief World Systems* in 1632 and *Discourses on Two Sciences* in 1638. In these works, he set out a range of scientific discoveries. Using a hand-crafted telescope, Galileo had been able to sketch the surface of the moon, observe the moons of Jupiter, record sunspots, and further distinguish between planets and stars. For his advocacy of the Copernican view of the universe (further verified by the mathematical calculations of Johannes Kepler) Galileo was forced—upon pain of excommunication—to declare that the earth and not the sun was at the center of the universe. For good measure, he was forced to spend the final decade of his life under virtual house arrest.

At the core of his work was the conviction that the structure of the physical world was not random. Galileo argued that the physical world operated according to a recognizable order and regular pattern. For this reason, variations in the physical world occurred in a consistent manner. This allowed for comparisons and generalizations. It also allowed for verification through experimentation. Galileo further argued that, given the fact that the physical world exhibited a consistent order and regular pattern, it was possible to view the physical world in a systematic manner that allowed scientists to describe this regular pattern according to precise mathematical formulas. In Galileo's words "the book of nature is written in mathematical language." Galileo developed mathematical laws for both the movement of the planets and the movement of bodies on Earth. Dropping cannonballs of unequal weight from the Leaning Tower of Pisa—the actual veracity of this story notwithstanding—was an example of Galileo's determination to experimentally test a hypothesis. His experimentation with falling bodies laid the groundwork for the modern practice of designing experiments to test hypotheses derived from mathematical formulas.

Toward this end, Galileo popularized an approach to scientific discovery known as the hypothetico-deductive method. The hypothetico-deductive method constructs an explanation by beginning with a mathematical hypothesis. A set of observable facts is then deduced from this hypothesis. This method was commonly used in the explanation of astronomical observations. For example, with both a phenomenal grasp of mathematics and rare access to the astronomical findings of his mentor, Tycho Brahe (1546–1601), Johannes Kepler (1571–1630) was able to accurately chart the elliptical orbit of the planets around the sun. A further example of the hypothetico-deductive method was the predicted return of Halley's comet in 1682. This prediction was based solely on two previous sightings in 1531 and 1607 and a set of algebraic equations.

Isaac Newton's *Mathematical Principles of Natural Philosophy* was published in 1687. Newton further championed the use of observation and experimentation along with the hypothetic-deductive method to understand the physical world. He exemplified the scientific method that began with observations supplemented by mathematical explanations. Such explanations, however, went far beyond the initial observations. Further claims—about what should be observed under certain circumstances—were inferred from the mathematical explanations and these were experimentally tested. To this point, the process was a purely empirical exercise driven by mathematical hypotheses.

However, what was observed and confirmed as true (or denied as false) by means of experiment went well beyond the immediate observation. Rather, these experimental observations represented an abstract mathematical explanation. This abstract explanation was the theory from which the experimental observations had been deduced. Theory supported by experimental findings was the foundation of Newtonian physics. Indeed, as one contributor to the development of positivism, Hans Reichenbach (1891–1953), argues in *The Rise of Scientific Philosophy* (1951), "mathematical deduction in combination with observation is the instrument that accounts for the success of modern science."

The basic principle was quite simple and very powerful. Under certain conditions one should observe certain phenomena. The bases for such predictions were (1) hypotheses concerning the influence of certain conditions on certain phenomena and (2) precise measurements of the conditions and the phenomena. Relationships between changes in the conditions and changes in the phenomena could be expressed in precise mathematical form. Take for example the simple phenomenon of water changing from a liquid to ice. It is observed that at a certain temperature (32 degrees Fahrenheit) water changes from liquid to ice. We observe that air temperature acts upon water in a certain way. We express this influence in mathematical form through a precise measurement of temperature and then state a general law for all similar cases: Under certain conditions (when the temperature is 32 degrees Fahrenheit or below) one should observe a certain phenomenon (water taking the form of ice).

This basic approach opened a myriad of possibilities for Newton. Building on Galileo's work with the laws of falling bodies, Newton demonstrated that all motion, whether on the earth or in the solar system, could be described by the same mathematical formulas. All matter moved as if every particle attracted every other particle with a force proportional to the product of the two masses, and inversely proportional to the square of the distance between them. The limitations of this general theory were not understood until discoveries in the field of quantum physics in the early twentieth century.

Additionally, breaking with a tradition dating back to Aristotle, Galileo refused to include a teleological explanation in his interpretation of the physical world. A teleological explanation is an argument based upon some notion of final causes or an underlying purpose. Prior to Galileo, teleological explanations had provided a crucial anchor to moral and ethical concerns. Specifically, the order and regularity in the physical world was understood to be evidence of God's master plan. To take credit for discovering the secrets of the physical world while denying God his fair due was utter heresy. (Newton himself felt compelled to add a brief commentary on the essential role of God in the design of the heavens in the third edition of *Mathematical Principles*.) Indeed, the current amoral posture of the physical sciences—generally taken for granted today—can be traced to Galileo. This separation of moral concerns from the technical procedures of physical science would have immense implications when efforts were later made to adapt such techniques for the social sciences.

WHAT ARE THE MAIN ELEMENTS OF EMBRYONIC POSITIVISM?

The main elements of embryonic positivism are not easily delineated. After all, embryonic positivism was, by definition, a fertile intellectual movement still in formation. Only the later, more fully formed version of positivism would yield a definitive set of rules and a properly rigid ideology. The main elements of embryonic positivism included distinct attitudes and beliefs alongside certain operations and techniques of investigation. The attitudes and beliefs reflected basic notions about the nature of the social world and about human activity in general. These thoughts were heavily influenced by the work of Bacon and Hume. The operations and techniques of investigation were developed to facilitate efforts to uncover deeper truths about the social world and human activity. These developments were framed by the ideas of Galileo and Newton. Embryonic positivism, struggling mightily to gain strength, was nourished to health by an able pair of nursemaids who rarely left its crib side, Auguste Comte and John Stuart Mill (1806–1873).

Comte, Mill, and the Main Elements of Embryonic Positivism

Comte's contributions to the social sciences are less important for the specific concepts and ideas underlying his project of uniting the physical and social sciences than for the enduring nature of the

21

project itself. Nonetheless, it is informative to outline Comte's positivist views in some detail so as to provide a bridge from the past to the present. Comte was clearly the most influential of the self-described positivist thinkers in the nineteenth century. The scope of the project he set out for himself and the zeal with which he pursued a purely positivist interpretation of the world have left deep impressions on contemporary approaches to social research.

Comte's views can be summarized as five basic principles. (1) Comte sought to adapt the successful methods of the physical sciences for the study of society and to unify all the branches of science through a common methodology based on empirical observation, comparisons of condition, experimentation, and quantitative calculation. (2) He held that the world consisted of observable, measurable phenomena (facts) and regulative patterns and relationships between phenomena (laws). (3) He rejected the search for ultimate purposes or the underlying nature (or essence) of phenomena as an activity outside the purview of science. (4) He believed that knowledge in all the branches of science unfolds in progressive stages, the final stage being positivism. (5) Lastly, Comte argued that the ultimate purpose of science was to promote social progress and order.

Comte published his six-volume *Course in Positive Philosophy* over a thirteen-year period from 1830 to 1842. This work was designed to launch society into a new era of understanding and social progress. The crowning achievement was going to be the development of a science of society, for which he coined the term "sociology." The ultimate goal was modest enough. Comte sought to subordinate all phenomena (both physical and social) under a single set of unifying laws and classificatory schemata. Quoting Comte from his *Course in Positive Philosophy*, "It is time to complete the vast intellectual project begun by Bacon, Descartes and Galileo by constructing the system of general ideas which must henceforth prevail among the human race." It is convenient to consider the five principles shaping Comte's work in the context of three issues that consumed a great deal of his time and energy: (1) the intrinsic links between the branches of science, (2) the three phases of human knowledge, and (3) the role of science in the organization of society.

Comte argued that there was a natural progression of human knowledge—evidenced by the history of scientific discovery—that could be traced across the scientific disciplines. This progression had begun in ancient Greece with the development of mathematics and would now be culminated with the work of Comte around sociology. There was a basic logic to Comte's argument. The emergence of each new branch of science was predicated on a body of previous scientific discoveries. The more complex sciences (biology, sociology), therefore, had to await the development of the less complex sciences (mathematics, astronomy).

Mathematics developed first because the type of knowledge that it generates—concerning quantitative relationships between phenomena—is the most general form of knowledge. It applies in the same manner to all phenomena. Mathematics is also the least complex, being reducible to rudimentary, quantitative measures of more or less. Comte argued that it was precisely because mathematics generated knowledge that was the most general and the least complex that it was discovered first. Conversely, sociology generated knowledge that was the least general and the most complex and, therefore, it could not have been discovered until all the other branches of science had been developed.

The evolution of knowledge in the various branches of science was orderly and logically arranged—as was the world they described. All of the branches were interlinked by a common process of discovery that relied upon previous laws governing a class of phenomena to generate new laws governing further classes of phenomena. Within this natural order there were two basic principles. First, the most general branches of science were developed before the least general branches. Second, those branches of science with the least complex subject matter were developed before those branches with the more complex subject matter. In this regard, knowledge itself was cumulative and knowledge in any one scientific branch stood in relation to knowledge in the other branches.

The discovery of astronomy followed that of mathematics. Astronomy was less general than mathematics (it applied only to celestial bodies) and added a degree of complexity with the concepts of mass and force to explain the relationships between objects in the sky. Physics followed astronomy at the end of the seventeenth century. Physics added further complexity by differentiating between types of force and introducing qualitative measures such as heat and light. Chemistry followed physics. The complexity of chemistry stemmed from its work with differentiated substances. The labors of Marie-François-Xavier Bichat (1771–1802), Georges Cuvier (1769–1839), and others next established the biological sciences, which were both the least general (with their focus on a narrow range of organic matter) and the most complex (with their greater number of qualities to account for). Following biology, in Comte's scheme, was sociology. Sociology was the summit of all the branches of science. It was both the least general and the most complex, and it was the development of sociology to which he dedicated his life's work.

The nature of human knowledge was itself a subject of study for Comte. He argued that knowledge had developed over time. Comte believed that the manner in which people interpreted and conceptualized the world had gone through specific stages of development. An essential part of human history was the history of developing a knowledge of the world. This occurred in three distinct phases—ending in positivism. Each phase was associated with different ways of understanding the world and distinct knowledge claims.

The first phase of human understanding was the theological period. All sciences initially passed through this period of primitive knowledge. In this era, people looked at the world around them and asked *why*. Superstition predominated, as people attributed magical or spiritual powers to the phenomena surrounding them. Comte argued that in the theological period people's viewpoints progressed from simple fetishism (objects themselves were treated as if they were alive and possessed their own feelings and purposes) to polytheism (different categories of phenomena were thought to be governed by different gods or spirits) to monotheism (the world was understood to be governed by one supreme being). The theological period was thus characterized by superstition; this was the earliest means by which observations and experiences about the world were organized.

The second phase of human understanding was the metaphysical period. *Why* remained the guiding question in this age, but superstition was replaced by secular (or natural) explanations of phenomena. Concepts such as "force," "essence," or "nature" replaced the direct role of God (though God might remain the original source of such metaphysical causes, the one initially setting them in motion). These concepts were metaphysical in the sense that their explanation lay beyond the physical world. They could not be immediately observed or experienced. Their prominence reflected an incomplete understanding of the world. Like Bacon before him, Comte attacked such metaphysical concepts as empty efforts to explain phenomena that people did not understand and that substituted for a true understanding of the world.

An oft cited example of the misguided use of metaphysical concepts at the time is the derisive comments of the French playwright Molière (1622–1673) on the idea that opium put people to sleep because of its "dormitive virtue." Comte shared Molière's belief that such notions were ludicrous and trite. With further investigation, he assured, one could discover the actual underlying causes of phenomena (the specific biological mechanisms accounting for the relationship between ingesting opium and falling asleep). Metaphysical causes (or hidden powers) were generally treated as a special kind of concept—such as "nature" or "essence." Thus, it was argued that it was the nature of opium to make people sleepy or that the essence of opium was its tendency to make people sleepy. Such reasoning was typical of the metaphysical period. Comte was adamant that what we knew—and all that we ever *could* know—about phenomena was their actual, outward appearance and not their mythical, inner essence. Human knowledge was limited to controlled observations about phenomena and did not extend to perhaps entertaining, but nonetheless baseless, speculation about the true nature or inner essence of phenomena. The third phase of human knowledge was born of this critique.

Positivism was the third phase of human knowledge. The most pronounced shift in the positivist era was that from the question of *why* to the question of *how*. This marked the death of metaphysical explanations and the birth of knowledge grounded in observation, comparison, experimentation, and calculation. In this regard, Comte followed closely on the heels of the British empiricists. The sole aim of the sciences was to discover the universal laws governing phenomena. This involved the systematic collection of—and submission to—facts. Pure deduction was rejected and concepts with no direct counterpart in the observable world were eliminated. The fundamental criterion of knowledge was its utility—its role in influencing and predicting events in the physical and social worlds.

Comte's conceptualization of knowledge and of science was referred to as phenomenalist. One did not blindly attempt to account for the underlying nature or essence of phenomena but investigated their actual manifestations in order to discover regular patterns that revealed the laws governing the relationships between phenomena. These laws encompassed the totality of all that we can know about the world. For instance, we know that gravity describes a relationship between bodies. But it would be pointless to ask, What *is* gravity? What is its essence? Comte argued that the human mind serves as a mirror of the objective reality. Our cumulative knowledge of this objective reality allows the mind to organize and order the range of phenomena.

The examples that Comte drew from to illustrate advances in the positivist period are taken from those sciences that had already reached this stage of development. Joseph Fourier (1768–1830), it was noted, had detailed the quantitative regularities of thermal phenomena without concern for the "true essence" of heat. Georges Cuvier examined the structure of organisms without reference to the nature of life. Newton developed his laws of gravity without fretting over the "essence" of matter or motion. Mathematics, astronomy, physics, chemistry, and biology had each reached the stage of positivism. This then made possible the next and final step—to discover the laws governing society.

The eventual development of a science of society would allow social life to be reconstructed on a rational basis. Science would, at last, serve as an instrument facilitating human control over both the physical and the social worlds. Because the last science to enter the positivist realm prior to sociology had been biology, Comte argued that strong analogies could be drawn between the two. He made direct comparisons between the categories of biological and sociological analysis. For instance, social differentiation—in the form of castes or classes—was likened to the differentiation of tissues in the body that made up various organs. Likewise, the heart, lungs, liver, and other organs of the body had their counterparts in society. The "organs" of society included the family, private property, religion, and language. Each organ's specific form could evolve and progress. However, its fundamental relationship to the other organs (its social role) remained fixed. The governing structure of these organs in society could change no more readily than those of the solar system or of the parts of the body.

Ultimately, Comte's vision entailed discovering and mapping an orderly and immutable classification system of the physical and social worlds. Individual phenomena were treated as members of larger classes of similar phenomena that stood in lawlike relation to other classes of phenomena. Positivism was the ultimate stage in the emancipation of reason—the final death of any knowledge claims linked to superstition or metaphysics.

Turning to the work of John Stuart Mill in the field of positivism, the record is a bit more mixed. With respect to his contributions to British empiricism and positivism, Mill is generally regarded less as an innovative thinker and more as a cogent synthesizer of previous debates. Prior to his more celebrated work in the areas of utilitarian ethics and liberty, Mill concerned himself extensively with methodological issues and the development of positivism. His renown in these fields tended to enhance his influence in other fields, such as methods.

His contributions to embryonic positivism were primarily in two areas: (1) his elaboration upon Bacon's inductive method with respect to the role of causal claims and (2) his consideration of the empiricists' critique of metaphysical reasoning and the nature of deductive reasoning. Mill's *System of Logic* was published in 1843, just one year after the sixth and final volume of Comte's *Course in Positive Philosophy*. Mill and Comte were familiar with one another's work. Indeed, aware at one point of Comte's dire personal finances, Mill had taken on the task of collecting funds in England to support his French colleague's efforts.

Much of Mill's early efforts went toward expanding upon Bacon's inductive methods. In particular, Mill attempted to establish an empirical basis for causal claims. He argued that by investigating similarities, differences, and parallel changes one could discover causal connections between phenomena. Many of his positivist peers disdained the notion of causation, arguing that the idea of "causal forces" implicitly suggested a form of metaphysical reasoning. To Mill, causation was a purely empirical matter. It referred to any instance when a certain phenomenon was observed to be a necessary and sufficient condition for another phenomenon to appear. We experience the world as a cascade of phenomena that appear to us as a series of individual impressions (or observations). For Mill, noting the sequence of observations—or the order by which phenomena appear—was no less empirical than the individual observation itself. This is what allows causal claims to be made that are based in (and verifiable through) empirical observation.

Mill also contributed to the empiricist critique of deduction. He argued that the deductive method—like its supposed contrast, the inductive method—was, in fact, entirely based on experience. The deductive method (as well as rationalism) was based on the belief that certain propositions, such as mathematical axioms, were not derived from experience. Mill rejected this claim. Rather, Mill argued that deductive reasoning was merely a device to simplify experience and to order observations. For example, if event B (dying) has always followed event A (drinking hemlock), then we may infer that event B (dying) will always follow event A (drinking hemlock).

This rudimentary example of deductive reasoning is based entirely upon observations of the two events. Indeed, even the elementary postulates of geometry can be shown to be merely the result of prolonged, systematic observation. There are, therefore, no truths whose alleged necessity can be established without appealing to observations. Importantly, Mill did not attempt to resolve the logical dilemma of inductive reasoning raised by Hume. As a result, by equating deductive reasoning with inductive reasoning, Mill was essentially arguing that any knowledge derived from either was equally without foundation. This had the troubling effect of simply burying the corpse of deductive reasoning alongside that of induction.

WHAT ARE THE IMPLICATIONS OF EMBRYONIC POSITIVISM?

It is genuinely difficult to overstate the impact of embryonic positivism on research practices in the social sciences today. While many surface-level details have evolved to give positivism a variety of flavors, a core set of underlying premises—originating in the era of embryonic positivism—has survived and remains a dominant influence across the social sciences. Each premise can be linked to a set of specific implications for scientific inquiry. Of particular influence have been five key premises.

(1) The first premise concerns the death of metaphysics and the triumph of empiricism as the foundation for all knowledge. The demise of metaphysics was not a quiet, victimless homicide. Metaphysical reasoning had been at the core of human understanding and interpretation of the world for countless centuries. Limiting all knowledge claims to those based on empiricism represented a mammoth sea change. Ultimate authority shifted from the church to the laboratory within a remarkably brief span of time. It was not that people no longer asked age-old philosophical questions about the meaning of life or the temperament of the gods. Rather, such questions were cordoned off from those scientific questions—such as the structure of the atom—about which one could reasonably hope to find truth with a high degree of certainty.

The implications of the death of metaphysics and the triumph of empiricism resulted, above all, in a narrowing of both the types of questions that could be asked and the manner in which questions could be framed. As discussed previously, embryonic positivists were adamant about asking *how* things worked rather than *why* they worked the way they did. The underlying nature of social interaction was less of a concern than the structure of social interaction. The meaning behind human action was a question beyond the scope of positivist science. The purpose of the social sciences was to predict and control human action. To do so, the social sciences had to break down all human activity (the actions of individuals or of groups) to its most minute constituent parts and to describe its basic parts and morphology.

(2) The second premise hailed the victory of comparison, experimentation, and the hypothetico-deductive method as the core research techniques of the social sciences. Debates among positivists, following the period of embryonic positivism, did not question the value of comparison and experimentation as ways of knowing. Rather, they focused simply on how to perfect techniques of comparison and experimentation. Discussions turned to the development of uniform standards and practices that followed precise and uniform rules. Within the social sciences today, research is carried out according to these rules and procedures for conducting comparisons of conditions or events in an exploratory manner or designing experiments to test theoretical claims based on the hypothetico-deductive method.

The implications of the victory of comparison and experimentation were twofold. First, this victory determined which subjects could be selected for study, and, second, it determined how research topics should be conceptualized for analysis. Because of this, certain types of human action were included and certain types excluded. To begin with, human actions suitable for study had to have qualities that were constant and fixed. Otherwise there would be nothing to compare. This implied that certain qualities, such as social norms, were sufficiently fixed that suppositions about them could be tested. In addition, all human action had to be measurable—both its duration and its quantitative dimensions. Otherwise, there would be no basis for comparisons. This implied that quantitative measures could be devised for qualitative concepts (such as social alienation, cultural assimilation, etc.). This led to the development of a sophisticated array of proxy variables (observable and measurable items that indicated the presence of a concept such as social alienation) in an effort to make possible the measurement of qualitative concepts.

Furthermore, all human action had to have certain features that were capable of being treated apart from other features. Otherwise, there would be no basis for conducting controlled experiments. This implied that it was possible to control for certain conditions (poverty, education, malnutrition) to test the influence of a specific factor (ethnicity) on a particular outcome (standardized test scores). It was assumed that the nature of all human action was such that humans would respond in a uniform, predictable manner to identical stimuli. Otherwise, there would be no basis for making generalizations from experimental findings. This implied that any isolated feature of society (racial prejudice) exposed to similar conditions (integrated communities) would yield the same results (racial tolerance or intolerance).

(3) The third premise was tied to the abandonment of absolute certainty as the standard of truth, contributing to a crisis in analysis among promoters of the inductive method and empiricism. The abandonment of absolute certainty as a standard of truth was an enormous shift. Previously there had been two standards of truth. The church reigned supreme because of its unique access to God and its exclusive rights to biblical interpretation and ritualistic gatekeeping. Beyond the church walls, rationalist Aristotelians had carved

out a second standard for truth based on rationalism and deductive logic. Beginning with Bacon's inductive method, the empiricists had been slowly chipping away at these sources of truth. The empiricists' advances in the areas of science and technology were indisputable. In the end, a pragmatic decision was taken. Absolute certainty in the realm of truth remained a laudable virtue. However, the material advances of the empiricists, combined with the fact that their methods did not rely upon a standard of absolute certainty, forced society to sacrifice absolute certainty on the altar of material progress.

The implications of abandoning absolute certainty as the standard of truth were many. Of particular concern were both the rise of statistical probability as a standard of truth and the debate over correlation versus causation. Returning to our green frogs, it was argued that the fact that all frogs thus far observed were green could serve as a fairly reliable indication that all future frogs would likewise be green. However, there remained the off chance that a red or purple one might turn up from time to time. Probability theory, as a standard of truth, argued that if we knew the total number of frogs in the world and the total number that had been randomly observed, we could mathematically determine the probability that the next frog we saw would also be green. The statistical likelihood of a condition or event occurring became the new standard of truth, rather than its actual certainty of occurring.

The shift from absolute certainty to probability also had implications for the notion of causation. Prior to this shift, causation had already raised a few eyebrows. To many, such as Hume, it was little more than a shadowy, metaphysical abstraction. The claim that event A (drinking hemlock) causes event B (death) simply because drinking hemlock has, until now, always preceded a person dying followed the same nebulous logic deployed by those observing that all frogs until now have been green. At best, it was argued, event A could be said to be strongly correlated with event B. Probability could be summoned to determine the likelihood of such an event occurring randomly or whether there seemed to be a link between the two and, with the aid of certain statistical calculations, one could generate a precise mathematical measure of likelihood. Strength of correlation rather than determinant causation became the measure of how different social processes were necessarily linked.

(4) The fourth premise celebrated the virtue of objectivity and the separation of moral concerns from techniques of investigation. Harking back to Bacon's Idols of the Cave, it became clear that a core mission of the revivalist empiricists was to embellish scientific inquiry with an ethic of rarefied indifference or pure objectivity. The researcher could have no stake or interest in the outcome of the investigation. The guiding motive was knowledge for knowledge's sake. Facts and laws had to be separated from ideology and politics. All observations and all research designs had to be fashioned in a manner that obscured the role of the observer (or researcher) to the greatest degree possible. Thus, all true techniques of investigation were considered to be inherently neutral and unbiased. All findings were to be relayed without value judgments.

The implications of treating the techniques of investigation as neutral and of separating moral considerations from scientific inquiry have proven to be, at times, harrowing. In an experiment conducted from the 1940s to the 1970s in Tuskegee, Alabama, scientists secretly withheld treatment for syphilis from a group of African American men so as to study the natural course of the illness. The study was carried out with the hope of advancing scientific knowledge and could only succeed if the scientists adhered to the strict rules of objectivity and indifference. Contrary to popular belief, this study was not a small, secretive conspiracy. Results from the study were published in prominent academic journals and presented at major medical conferences throughout the 1960s. Thus, a great many fellow researchers from across the scientific community were aware of and anxiously following this study throughout its duration. The separation of moral considerations from scientific inquiry was so complete that no objection was ever raised by the scientific community. Ethical concerns were not raised until a newspaper article first questioned the study in the early 1970s.

(5) The fifth premise argued that the proper measure of the true worth of any scientific knowledge was its contribution to progress and technological advance. It had, after all, been largely on the basis of the startling, innovative advances made possible by the scientific method in the sixteenth and seventeenth centuries that embryonic positivism had relegated all previous forms of investigation to the dustbin of history. The purpose of science, therefore,

along with knowledge for knowledge's sake, was to foster material and social progress. Those forms of knowledge contributing to the development of modern society were held up as great achievements in social evolution while those holding society back were greatly disparaged as backward and barbaric. Accordingly, societies that adopted the most modern and proven ways of thinking were considered the most advanced civilizations. Other societies languished as undeveloped and technologically (and socially) primitive civilizations. A society's ready acceptance of the scientific method as the definitive test of knowledge claims was taken as a sign of sophistication and modernity. It is noteworthy that this programmatic commitment to progress (as a measure of worthiness) somewhat contradicted the previous claims to complete objectivity and indifference.

The implications of measuring the worth of scientific knowledge by its contribution to progress and technological advance are varied and demonstrate, perhaps to a greater extent than the previous premises, the degree to which the foundations of embryonic positivism have directly affected fundamental political and moral questions across society. Because the most highly valued knowledge was that which advanced technological progress, any forms of knowledge that contributed to nontechnical advances in society (knowledge related to social values or cultural ethics for example) were less valued. This had a profound impact by privileging certain values and perspectives that tended to promote the interests of persons in power who benefited from the given social order based on technical and material progress.

As has been frequently noted, non-Western cultures often value things other than technical and material progress. Social harmony and respect for tradition may enjoy greater value than patterns of social and technical development that disrupt established social relationships. Certain social roles with no specialized knowledge claims are often less valued in materially advanced societies than in materially less developed societies. Such roles include women as nurturers or elders as community leaders and intergenerational links. The unique knowledge associated with these social roles is often not validated in materially advanced Western societies. Thus, while many advanced Western societies set off along a development path that looked to technological progress as the measure of modern civilization, many non-Western societies (and many marginal communities within advanced Western societies) pursued equal social advances with measures linked to other values.

The implications of embryonic positivism have been undeniably profound and far-reaching. The next chapter explores further developments in the field of positivism—specifically the field of logical positivism—that sought to clarify and sharpen certain issues and questions while deepening these five premises and broadening their implications.

FURTHER READING

Benton, Ted, and Ian Craib. "Empiricism and Positivism in Science." Pp. 13–28 in *Philosophy of Social Science*. New York: Palgrave, 2001.

Halfpenny, Peter. "Comte and the Early Period." Pp. 13–27 in *Positivism and Sociology*. London: George Allen and Unwin, 1982.

Kolakowski, Leszek. "Auguste Comte: Positivism in the Romantic Age." Pp. 45–70 in *The Alienation of Reason: A History of Positivist Thought*. Garden City, N.J.: Doubleday, 1969.

Marcuse, Herbert. "Foundations of Positivism and the Rise of Sociology." Pp. 323–89 in *Reason and Revolution: Hegel and the Rise of Social Theory*. Boston: Beacon Press, 1966.

Simon, Walter. "Auguste Comte and Positivism." Pp. 3–19 in *European Positivism in the Nineteenth Century*. Ithaca, N.Y.: Cornell University Press, 1963.

2

Logical Positivism

WHAT IS LOGICAL POSITIVISM?

The first three chapters of this book concern the evolution of positivism as a distinct research orientation in the social sciences. Each chapter details a unique moment in the history of positivism. For this reason, chapters 2 and 3 are cumulative. They expand and build upon the previous chapters. At one level, therefore, the discussion of logical positivism is broader than that of embryonic positivism insofar as it incorporates and embellishes the previous history. At another level, however, the discussion of logical positivism is narrower than that of embryonic positivism. This is because those associated with logical positivism represented a more coherent and cohesive gang of intellectuals than those associated with embryonic positivism. This resulted in the pursuit of a common project with a relatively well-defined focus.

The purpose of this chapter, therefore, is to examine logical positivism as a distinct moment in the long life of positivism. At the core of logical positivism is a near-obsessive focus on the use of language within scientific inquiry. This grew out of a simmering disquiet in the early twentieth century regarding the meaning and validity of scientific statements. The problem was no longer determining what was true and what was false. The problem was finding a meaningful and universal language to convey what was true and what was false. In this regard, the work of Ernst Mach (1838–1916) and Richard Avenarius (1843–1896) in the realm of empiricism and that of Bertrand Russell (1872–1970) in the realm of logic provide essential bridges between nineteenth-century embryonic positivism and twentieth-century logical positivism. As evidence of the varied and at times confusing interpretations of positivism in the latter nineteenth century, all three of these contributors actively dissociated themselves from the term "positivist."

All of the issues and debates discussed in this chapter can be considered foundational for the practice of standard social science research today. Of all the chapters of this book, however, the present chapter concerns an intellectual movement whose proponents made the fewest explicit links to the social sciences. The early proponents of logical positivism took the physical sciences as their immediate subject of concern. It was not until later, by means of gradual extension, that the arguments of logical positivism were systematically applied to the social sciences.

WHAT ARE THE ORIGINS OF LOGICAL POSITIVISM?

Logical positivism emerged, in large measure, from the gallant efforts of Ernst Mach and Richard Avenarius to purge the last surviving remnants of subjectivity from scientific inquiry. Of particular concern was the extent to which the individual characteristics of an investigator were allowed to influence a study's results. Such results would be unique to the individual investigator and thus would not constitute a general finding—the essential building block of scientific knowledge. Efforts to eliminate the influence of the individual investigator within scientific inquiry are referred to as empiriocriticism.

The goal of empiriocriticism is to represent phenomena as they truly are, through "pure experience"—untainted by the role of the investigator. Importantly, proponents of logical positivism do not advocate a retreat to pure objectivism. This would suggest a utopian vision, completely separating the investigator from the research process. Rather, there is an attempt to clearly define and narrowly circumscribe the role of the investigator within scientific inquiry. Within this framework, the investigator does not represent a passive reflection of reality but remains an active agent in the production of knowledge.

Bertrand Russell's concerns are less with the nature of scientific inquiry as a process and more with the representation of the scientific findings in a meaningful language as they emerge from this process. The field of logic within philosophy concerns the structure of formal arguments. An argument consists of a series of statements (or propositions) and a conclusion that logically follows from these statements. An argument is valid when its conclusion can be logically deduced from its propositions. Russell demonstrated that it was actually the form of the argument—rather than the truth of the statements—that determines whether an argument is valid. Thus logic is a tool available to scientific inquiry whose validity cannot be influenced by the content of the study. This insight had a profound impact on the development of logical positivism.

Ernst Mach and Richard Avenarius

Though laboring independently, Mach and Avenarius pursued the common goal of merging philosophy and science. Both believed that the central purpose of philosophy is to analyze the conceptual structure and language that science uses to synthesize and interpret its findings. Though sharing this common project, each pursued distinct interests. Mach, with a rich appreciation for experimental and theoretical physics, remained steeped in the process of scientific inquiry. Avenarius, with a greater concentration on philosophical traditions, remained fascinated by the possibility of a unified scientific view of the world.

While Mach sought insight from his extensive study of the history of physics, Avenarius sought to demonstrate that all of the concepts that are specific to individual branches of science can be linked to more general, unifying concepts that reflect the totality of knowledge. Their work converges around several themes, including the precise application of language to scientific inquiry. Each sought to establish universal criteria for judging the meaning and validity of scientific statements. Mach and Avenarius made two major contributions to the development of logical positivism: their revision of empiricism to minimize subjectivity and the principle of economy.

Revising empiricism and exorcising subjectivity

Over several decades, a series of major advances in the physical sciences—most prominently Nikolai Lobachevsky's (1793–1856) non-

Euclidean geometry, developments in quantum mechanics, and Albert Einstein's (1879–1955) theory of relativity—had weakened the empirical foundation of the physical sciences. It was no longer tenable to conceive of geometry, for example, as a science of a priori synthetic truths concerning observable spatial phenomena. An a priori synthetic truth is an empirical fact that a person somehow knows prior to any experience with that fact. Mach and Avenarius grew leery of the increasing tendency of the physical sciences to use terms that had no direct connection to observable phenomena.

Mach's interpretation of empiricism in this regard was uncompromising. He was a radical antidogmatist in the Humean tradition. Because he believed that all claims must remain open to criticism, Mach regarded all scientific conclusions as, at best, provisional. Like Avenarius, he rejected any search for the inner essence of phenomena or any a priori conditions for their existence. Furthermore, Mach argued that there was no meaningful distinction to be made between the ordinary language of everyday experience and the language of scientific inquiry. The language of science organizes empirically acquired observations, while ordinary language organizes observations from everyday experience. Both represent systems for organizing experience as shaped by cognitive processes (the act of thinking). These cognitive processes, it was believed, are ultimately governed by physiological processes.

These thoughts are most fully explored in Mach's two major works, *The Science of Mechanics* (1883) and *The Analysis of Sensation* (1886), and Avenarius's *Critique of Pure Experience*, published between 1888 and 1890. These core works of empiriocriticism seek to analyze the process by which one can somehow separate the actual "true" world of observed phenomena from those aspects of one's understanding of such phenomena that are added by the investigator. To better understand this process, both Mach and Avenarius developed a physiological description of how one perceives phenomena.

Mach's and Avenarius's interpretation of empiricism begins with an exploration of precisely how one experiences the world. All human cognition concerns a response of the organism (the human being) to a "disturbance" of its biological balance. Imagine you are in a room with no light or sound and the door is suddenly thrown open. The light from the hall and the sound of a door opening can be considered a disturbance to your biological balance. Mach and Avenarius assert that your response to such a disturbance will be shaped by the same laws that govern all physiological processes. This analysis extends beyond momentary disturbances (such as a door suddenly thrown open) and applies to all cognitive acts (all conscious thinking). Thus, Mach and Avenarius reduce cognition to a basic physiological process associated with the central nervous system.

At the same time, the content of cognition (what we know about what we experience) is not limited to the immediate circumstances in which we find ourselves. This is where things get tricky. Each of us has a stored-up collection of past experiences, beginning from the day we were born. These past experiences shape the content of our current experiences. We rely on past experience to understand, for instance, that we are in a room connected to a hallway and that someone has just opened the door to the hallway. Thus, from a purely physiological perspective, experience is nothing more than a combination of perceptions that are organized into collections of impressions that allow us to navigate the everyday world. When you wake each morning, you rely upon a series of physiological processes to guide you through your morning routine based upon a store of information gathered through past experience.

Notice that Mach and Avenarius are allowing an important qualification to "pure" empiricism. A person's understanding of a given phenomenon is not limited to immediate sense perceptions. Rather, immediate sense perceptions—what Mach refers to as "elements"—are filtered and interpreted through a store of previous experiences. This is the task of cognition. Cognition allows us to refer to elements as specific phenomena (a chair, a table, a dog, etc.) insofar as our past experience allows us to link the elements in permanent, recurring combinations.

New knowledge, scientific or otherwise, is generated through the interaction of the fixed residues of old impressions gathered through experience—what Avenarius refers to as "apperceptive masses"—and previously unencountered phenomena. Apperceptive masses play an active role in shaping how new phenomena are taken in and processed. They select components from the large store of accumulated experiences to make sense of what one is experiencing at any given moment. Through a series of cognitive processes, the mind endows the new phenomena with meaning based on its store of familiar phenomena. Both our recognition of previously encountered phenomena and our incorporation of new-ly experienced phenomena are, therefore, attributable to physiolog-ical processes that shape and maintain our permanent images of the world.

It is important for Mach and Avenarius to establish that cognition can be reduced to purely physiological processes so as to prepare us for the next step of applying this to the process of scientific inquiry. This is, ultimately, what makes possible the very notion of scientific inquiry with a muted subjectivity. In this respect, the world of the scientist represents a collection of perceptions and apperceptive masses suitable for constructing scientific concepts. Scientists are able to uncover laws and theories governing the world of phenomena via scientific inquiry (observation and experi-mentation) alone because scientific inquiry consists entirely of those cognitive processes associated with the exposure of new phenomena to the apperceptive masses of properly trained scientists.

In this way, scientists are able to merely describe the world of phenomena without *adding* anything to the description that is not found in experience. The empirical sciences tell us nothing about the world that does not originate in experience. Once one has described a given phenomenon in as great a detail as possible, there is nothing left to be explained. Therefore, it is held, there is no distinction between the description of phenomena and the ex-planation of phenomena.

Principle of economy

Mach and Avenarius maintain that we can only assert the existence of those phenomena that are actually based in experience. Conse-quently, any phenomena that are not derived from experience must be eliminated from our vocabulary. In this sense, we must attempt to economize our description of the world. The principle of econ-omy describes an unconscious, regulative physiological process that shapes our interpretation and incorporation of experience. It is believed that the principle of economy reflects the actual behavior of the central nervous system when one interacts with phenomena.

The history of scientific advance has been the history of constant economizing, bringing science closer and closer to knowledge based on pure experience. Over time, those elements not present in pure experience (such as values or essences) have been discarded. The principle of economy merely describes a physiological law that governs the assimilation of new cognitive content. It is the criterion by which cognitive processes—governed by our central nervous system—determine which concepts to incorporate. By way of example, Mach argues that the role of concepts or theories in scientific inquiry is both to economize on language and to share acquired experience through a common idiom so that each investigator is not required to constantly experiment individually. Science is experience, economically ordered. The use of concepts presents a ready example of the principle of economy. The concept of a river enjoys a widely shared understanding. Use of the concept *river* serves as shorthand for certain recurrent characteristics that are manifested in a series of repeated experiences that each of us has. In this way we are not forced to constantly describe in full detail what we mean when referring to a river in everyday conversation. We can say, "I walked along the river," rather than having to say, "I walked along the winding channel of water full of fish and silt that is connected to a large body of water."

At the same time, Mach and Avenarius recognized that it is not entirely possible to construct scientific statements without the use of terms that are not linked to sensory perception in the strict empirical sense. Mach treated such terms—such as the concept of "force" in physics—as auxiliary devices to help economize on language. These were distinguished from terms that were references to a specific empirical phenomenon—for example, a falling rock. Auxiliary devices, therefore, aid in the organization of scientific thought. Mach argued that such auxiliary devices are permissible so long as they are always traceable, in the final analysis, to empirical phenomena. The language of science, therefore, consists of two types of words. Words belonging to the first type are the product of empirical observation. Words of the second type are auxiliary devices that—though not directly observable—are grounded in the world of observable phenomena. For logical positivists, this was a less-than-satisfactory resolution.

Bertrand Russell

Bertrand Russell's major contributions to the development of logical positivism are in the field of logic. These can be summarized as three basic insights. Along with his development of relational logic (which allowed for hypothetical statements), Russell demonstrated that the validity of an argument is based on its form and not on the truth of its propositions and that mathematics is in fact a subfield of logic and not an empirical science (such as physics or biology). Between 1910 and 1913, Russell published *Principia Mathematica* in collaboration with Alfred Whitehead (1861–1947). Most of these insights were first explored here. Prior to this monumental work, few substantive innovations had been made to the original logic of Aristotle. (The only major exception to this was the contribution to mathematical logic by Gottlob Frege [1848–1925] in the latter nineteenth and early twentieth century.)

The central concern of logic is the construction of valid reasoning through argumentation. Arguments consist of a series of statements (or propositions) leading to conclusions. Russell sought to establish, first, the conditions under which propositions are valid in relation to other propositions and, second, the conditions under which one proposition may be deduced (or inferred) from another proposition. He built his findings largely upon his work with the logic of mathematical propositions in which he demonstrated that the entirety of mathematics could be derived from a small number of logical axioms. Russell wondered whether the same principle might hold true for language; if it did, a purely logical language might be possible that would express everything that could be stated.

Validity of an argument determined by its form

Russell began by distinguishing between the truth of an argument's propositions and the validity of the argument overall. It was an argument's form—and not the truth of its propositions—that determined the validity of the argument. An argument's propositions may be false and the argument can still be valid. For this reason, the proper focus of logic is the validity of an argument (the accuracy of its form) and not the truth of its propositions. Russell maintained that when the conclusion of an argument is implied by the argument's propositions, then the argument is valid. However, when the conclusion of an argument is implied by the argument's propositions *and* the argument's propositions are true, then the argument is sound.

Consider the following argument.

If neither Guillermo nor Diego has ever been to Fargo, then Diego has never been to Fargo.

The argument itself is valid regardless of whether Guillermo or Diego has ever been to Fargo. If it is also true that neither Guillermo nor Diego has ever been to Fargo, then the argument is both valid and sound. The example further illustrates why logical relationships are necessarily true and cannot be falsified through empirical observation. In this sense, logic is empty of content. It is precisely because logic (and by extension mathematics) is empty of content—and thus incapable of introducing bias—that it is so valuable for scientific inquiry. Logic can never falsify a scientific finding because it cannot introduce any new content.

Relational logic

On the basis of the preceding discussion, it is clear that an argument is comprised of a set of propositions with links. These links create inferences between propositions. The classic example is:

All P's are Q's. All Q's are R's. Therefore all P's are R's.

The formal logic developed by Russell attempts to identify networks of propositions within arguments and to test the validity of the inferences between propositions. This innovation greatly expands the types of arguments that can be studied beyond Aristotle's syllogisms. It will be recalled from chapter 1 that a syllogism is a type of argument based upon a major premise, a minor premise, and a conclusion that follows therefrom. Aristotle's logic only pertains to descriptive predicates that classify things. Arguments are restricted to propositions describing the qualities of phenomena.

Under the old logic there is no way to infer relationships. For example, one cannot argue the following:

If Maria is the mother of Gabriela, then Gabriela is the daughter of Maria.

Russell's new logic included relational predicates. The rules for determining the validity of deductions from relational propositions are inferential. We indicate relational inferences through the use of terms such as "and" and "or." Arguments could now describe relationships *between* phenomena. (For example: The blue car is larger than the green car.)

Russell's new logic also made possible the development of hypothetical propositions, which are a central component of scientific inquiry. These are commonly referred to as "if ... then statements." There are two principal forms of hypothetical statements. The method of affirming (or *modus ponens*) is the simplest form of conditional statement. For example:

> *Conditional Statement 1:* If A (the car crashes) then B (it will make a sound).
> *Conditional Statement 2:* It is the case that A (the car does crash).
> *Conclusion:* Therefore, B (there is a sound).

The method of denying (*modus tollens*) takes a slightly different form. If a conditional proposition is held to be true but its consequent is false, then the conditional proposition must also be false. For example:

> *Conditional Statement 1:* If and only if A (I walk across the room) then B (my feet will touch the floor).
> *Conditional Statement 2:* However, not B (my feet did not touch the floor).
> *Conclusion:* Therefore, not A (I could not have walked across the room).

For arguments linked to either the method of affirming or the method of denying, it is the form of the argument that determines its validity. Importantly for the development of logical positivism, it was therefore now possible to assume that any statement that is implied by the premises of an argument can be considered to have been explained.

Mathematics as a subfield of logic

The third major contribution of Russell to the development of logical positivism concerns the reduction of mathematics to a branch of logic. Mathematics could, therefore, no longer be treated as an empirical science. The truth of mathematical claims is a critical consideration for logical positivists, who place great emphasis on empirical evidence. Rendering mathematics—whose truths are a crucial cornerstone of scientific inquiry—a branch of logic has had the effect of eliminating the need to find empirical support for mathematical claims. Mathematics as a whole is viewed as a system of relationships between propositions that are derived from postulated axioms. Thus, mathematics is a logical system, reliant only upon internal references, that is held together by a series of tautological deductions.

Non-Euclidean geometry had already demonstrated that geometry could not be viewed as a simple description of patterns in the universe. Rather, geometry is a logical system of interrelated propositions that cannot be empirically verified. The importance of this finding is that synthetic statements (empirically derived statements) can be limited to sense data and that the realm of scientific inquiry can encompass both empirical sense data and logical relationships.

What Are the Main Elements of Logical Positivism?

Logical positivism brought together a loose band of philosophers and scientists (largely Austrian) who made up a major intellectual movement in the 1920s and 1930s. Given the concentration of its founding members at the University of Vienna, this group was referred to as the Vienna Circle. In tribute to its intellectual lineage, until 1929 it was called the Ernst Mach Society. In 1922, the group's organizer, Moritz Schlick (1882–1936), took over the chair in the philosophy of science at the University of Vienna, a post that had been held by Mach since 1896. The link to Mach was somewhat ironic. Members of the Vienna Circle placed a far greater emphasis on the presentation of the results of scientific inquiry than on the actual process of scientific inquiry. Mach had generally emphasized both. Thus, of those in the Vienna Circle (see list below), only three—Moritz Schlick, Hans Reichenbach, and Phillip Frank—had formal training in experimental physics. In many ways, the basic orientation of the Vienna Circle represented an approach closer to that of Avenarius than Mach.

Beyond Schlick, the other Vienna-based members included Rudolf Carnap (1891–1970), Herbert Feigl (1902–1973), Phillip Frank

(1884–1966), Kurt Gelling (1886–1942), Kurt Gödel (1906–1978), Hans Hahn (1879–1934), Otto Neurath (1882–1945), and Friedrich Waisman (1896–1960). Other significant contributors included Carl Hempel (1905–1997) and Hans Reichenbach (1891–1953) in Berlin and Alfred Ayer (1910–1989) in England. Key works from members of the Vienna Circle include two edited volumes, *A Scientific World-View: The Vienna Circle* (1929) and *Unified Science* (1938); Carnap's *Logical Structure of the World: Pseudoproblems in Philosophy* (1928); Neurath's *Empirical Sociology* (1931); Schlick's *Problems in Ethics* (1939); and Ayer's *Language, Truth, and Logic* in 1936. This last work was, in fact, the introduction of logical positivism to the English-speaking world.

Proponents of logical positivism began with a rather unsettling premise. They contended that there had been a grave misunderstanding among philosophers over the centuries regarding the true nature of philosophy. A great many superfluous issues had been allowed to enter the field. This had inevitably led to pointless metaphysical speculation. The task of philosophy in the twentieth century had to be limited to the analysis of precisely how people used language to describe and explain the world around them. The Vienna Circle's goal was the establishment of a purely objective and neutral language of observation. Their most immediate focus was the language of scientific inquiry within the physical sciences. However, being quite generous of spirit, logical positivists offered, once and for all, to sort out all the messy philosophical debates that had taken up so much time over the centuries. In this regard they were able to establish that all philosophical questions fall into one of two categories. Either they are metaphysical—What is the meaning of life? Is there an afterlife?—in which case they are nonsensical and an utter waste of time, or they are analytical—What is the organic composition of the human body? What is the rate of decomposition of the human body following death?—in which case they are of great importance and worthy of painstaking study.

Taking their cue from Avenarius, the Vienna Circle maintained that the most fundamental task of logical positivism is to establish a foundational language and a set of rules for unifying all of the physical and social sciences. If the physical sciences seem further advanced than the social sciences, this is merely due to a greater maturity on the part of the former. However, all of the achievements of the physical sciences are but a mirror of the certain path of the social sciences in generations to come. The first step—which the logical positivists took upon themselves to begin—was to examine the logical content of statements within physics, one of the most advanced branches of the physical sciences.

This unity of all fields of knowledge lay behind the need to first categorize all scientific inquiries as either metaphysical or analytical in nature and to then systematically eliminate the former. Metaphysical inquiries are not only logically confused, they are, in fact, meaningless. This is simply because the logical content of any statement that is not grounded in observation and experience cannot be judged. Therefore, philosophy was freed from having to waste its time on such matters. The task of philosophy was now to narrowly focus on the manner by which the language of scientific inquiry logically reported scientific results. Two major developments emerged from this campaign: (1) the verification principle and (2) the move from phenomenalism to physicalism (and the triumph of inter-subjective agreement). Before taking up these concerns, however, it is necessary to briefly turn to a hotly debated philosophical work that greatly influenced the development of logical positivism.

The Contributions of Wittgenstein

Though Ludwig Wittgenstein (1898–1951) was not actively involved with the Vienna Circle, his work was considered essential by many members. Of particular interest was his *Tractatus Logico-Philosophicus* (1922). Wittgenstein had been a student of Bertrand Russell. Reflecting the influence of Russell, Wittgenstein sought to combine the rules of logic with the limitations of empiricism so as to delineate the manner by which we experience and understand phenomena. *Tractatus* maintains that sense perception is our only way to experience the world. Through sense perceptions we accumulate individual facts about the world. These individual facts are expressed through "atomic sentences." Thus, the content of our entire knowledge about the world is reducible to a description of these individual facts. Importantly, we can know nothing beyond our sense perceptions, and the language we develop to describe the world must not go beyond this. "The limits of my language are the limits of my world" is a popular aphorism from *Tractatus*.

A second argument from *Tractatus* is that, while we can ask whether a certain fact belongs to the world as we experience it, we cannot ask meaningful questions about the world as a whole. We are limited to building up atomic statements that reflect individual facts. The manner by which *Tractatus* limits all meaningful statements to descriptions of individual facts raises certain difficulties concerning the use of nonempirical concepts that refer to abstract groupings of individual facts—for example, the notion of "horses." Consider the following three statements.

(1) The horse in the barn has four legs.
(2) The three horses in the field are running.
(3) Horses are warm-blooded.

Statement 1 refers to an observable phenomenon that is verifiable, a specific horse in the barn. Statement 2 refers to observable phenomena that are verifiable, three specific horses in the field. Statement 3 does not refer to any directly observable phenomena. It refers to the concept of "horses." The statement is true; however, it is not verifiable via observation and experience. It is therefore not considered a meaningful statement and, according to the *Tractatus*, it is not permissible as a description of the world.

The Verification Principle

Building upon Wittgenstein's basic insights, members of the Vienna Circle set out to develop precise procedures for describing the world. They based such descriptions on so-called protocol sentences. Protocol sentences are descriptions of sense perception with nothing added. These are what Wittgenstein referred to as atomic sentences. Linking observations from the physical world with propositions (or theories) about the physical world presented a major challenge. A complex system of correspondence rules was designed to translate back and forth between the language of observation and the language of theory. Such formulations raise certain difficulties. There is a fundamental dilemma regarding the links between protocol sentences and propositions about the world. It is simply not a practical or realistic expectation that one trace all the propositions used in scientific inquiry to specific protocol sentences.

Many propositions about the world emerge from random inspiration or wild fits of speculation. Such conjectures are then framed as hypotheses and tested. The original propositions, therefore, are quite frequently not directly linked to observation and experience. However, to abandon this link between propositions about the world and observations of the world is to sever scientific inquiry from observation and experience. This was not acceptable. From this dilemma emerged the verification principle. The verification principle holds that a statement is meaningful only if it can be verified. Technically stated, the meaning of a statement is tied to the process by which it is verified. Propositions are considered meaningful if they can serve as potential premises of protocol sentences. In other words, one should be able to develop and test hypotheses (or predictions) based on the formulation of the proposition. Take the following propositions by way of example.

(1) When someone dies, his or her body's carbon content disintegrates.
(2) When someone dies, his or her soul joins the angels in heaven.

Members of the Vienna Circle argued that proposition 1 is testable following a person's death whereas proposition 2 is not. Therefore, only proposition 1 can be said to be meaningful.

The verification principle was also enlisted to resolve a troubling discrepancy between specific statements and general statements (or predictions). Consider the following statements.

(1) There is a car in the street.
(2) All cars driven in the street have wheels.

Statement 1 is specific and verifiable through observation and experience. Statement 2 is neither specific (all cars) nor irrefutably verifiable. It refers to an indefinite number of cars. The verifiability of statement 2 is limited because any car driven in the street without wheels at some time in the future would invalidate the statement. Statement 2 represents a general statement—the type used for prediction. There is no single fact that can verify a general statement such as this. Therefore, according to the verification principle, it is a meaningless statement. However, such general statements are the bases for making predictions, and making predictions

represents the very soul of scientific inquiry. This forced proponents of logical positivism to include statements that were capable
of verification on the basis of a high degree of probability. The
refinement of rules for probabilistic statements was further advanced by a later generation following in the footsteps of logical
positivism in the 1940s and 1950s.

The Move from Phenomenalism to Physicalism

A further issue regarding the use of protocol sentences concerned
the subjective nature of an observer's individual experience. Logical
positivists were much alarmed by the difficulty of distinguishing
between contradictory reports of the same phenomena. The initial
consensus of the Vienna Circle regarding the standard of truth of
statements was referred to as phenomenalism. (This is not to be
confused with phenomenology, a major school of thought that is
discussed in later chapters.) Phenomenalism is the belief that all
meaningful statements must be restricted to those that describe
immediate sense perception (Wittgenstein's atomic statements). This
presents a basic dilemma. If meaningful statements are limited to
sense perceptions as they are recorded in each individual's consciousness, then how can one verify the authenticity of each private
experience? If I say that I see three ducks on the pond and you say
that you see two ducks on the pond—or that you see a walrus
flying across the sky, for that matter—how are we to determine
whose sense perception is accurate?

The inherent difficulty of determining the authenticity of conflicting
private experiences led by the mid-1930s to a dramatic shift from
phenomenalism to a new consensus favoring physicalism. Physicalism
is the belief that all meaningful statements must be restricted to those
that refer to commonly experienced phenomena in a shared environment. According to the principles of phenomenalism, statements refer
to sense perceptions in our private experience. An example of such a
statement is: I see two ducks on the pond. According to the principles
of physicalism, statements refer to phenomena that are commonly
experienced in the world. An example of such a statement is: All
persons who are present see two ducks on the pond.

While clarifying certain discrepancies, physicalism also signaled
a further move away from absolute, certain truth. Instead, the new

standard of truth for scientific inquiry—based on physicalism—became intersubjective agreement. Intersubjective agreement holds that a statement is meaningful if it refers to phenomena that are commonly experienced by a general community of observers. This, of course, leaves open the potential for collective delusion and thus cannot guarantee absolute, certain truth. Thus, beginning in the 1930s, all meaningful statements within scientific inquiry had to refer to physical phenomena—based on sense perception—that could be publicly verified. This remains the cardinal standard of truth for the dominant methodological approaches in both the physical and social sciences to this day.

WHAT ARE THE IMPLICATIONS OF LOGICAL POSITIVISM?

Most of the premises and implications of embryonic positivism discussed in chapter 1 can be easily extended to logical positivism. It is helpful, therefore, to distinguish those features unique to logical positivism as a specific, evolutionary form of positivism in general. For this, the main principles of logical positivism can be organized around five premises. Each premise entails a specific set of implications.

(1) The first premise of logical positivism concerns the language for expressing knowledge. True knowledge is limited to two types of statements: (1) statements that are descriptions of direct observations (empiricism) and (2) statements that are linked via the logic of deduction to descriptions of direct observations (rationalism). Judging all knowledge by empirical and rationalist criteria was a further attempt to cast off the metaphysical mischief makers from the world of scientific inquiry.

One rather troubling implication of this premise—linked to the empirical nature of all true statements—concerns the difficulty of conceptualizing group (rather than individual) characteristics. A major challenge for those attempting to apply logical positivism to the social sciences has always been the nature of so-called social wholes. A social whole is a concept representing an abstract collection of specific things. This follows from Wittgenstein's discussion of how to account for abstract concepts such as "horses." It will be recalled that Wittgenstein argued that there is a fundamental difference between statements referring to two or three specific horses and statements referring to the general category of horses. This difficulty is exemplified by attempts to deal with social wholes in the social sciences.

Sociology, for instance, is often concerned with social groups such as African American professors, the Mormon community, or rural youth. Such "wholes" are not reducible to protocol sentences. They do not represent specific, observable phenomena. You can observe individual Mormons but you cannot "observe" the entirety of the Mormon community. One approach to resolving this dilemma has been the school of behaviorism in psychology. Behaviorism reduces all human behavior to its most minute, basic forms, based on the physiological needs of the human organism interacting with its environment.

Otto Neurath attempted to extend the principles of behaviorism to sociology and to characterize all social wholes as complex aggregates of member traits. Paul Lazersfeld (1901–1976), an occasional participant in the Vienna Circle, built on this work in the 1950s and 1960s. Lazersfeld represented social groups as complex aggregates of sets of variables that measured different features of a group. Meaningful statements about the Mormon community as a whole can be developed by analyzing individual-level traits of a sample of Mormons. Mormons as a whole can never be observed. However, because the Mormon community is conceived of as nothing more than the aggregate of its members, various features of the social group can be measured.

(2) The second premise of logical positivism is that the primary purpose of scientific inquiry is to generate a network of knowledge statements that are linked by deductive logic. Such statements are grounded in prior statements that are descriptions of direct observation. Scientific inquiry must, therefore, dedicate itself to the development of complex networks of interrelated knowledge statements. The rationale for this follows directly from the first premise. The basic assertion is therefore painfully uninteresting. However, the more general programmatic claim of the second premise—that the construction of networks of knowledge statements is the primary purpose of scientific inquiry—warrants further consideration.

The emphasis on rationally derived networks of knowledge statements represents a subtle shift in the era of logical positivism regarding the nature of knowledge and truth. In embryonic positivism, a great premium had been placed on the development of knowledge that contributes to social progress. This is an instrumentalist view of knowledge, represented by Francis Bacon's proclamation that "knowledge is power." The literal meaning of Bacon's claim is that the proper criterion for judging "true" knowledge is its proven utility. In Bacon's eyes, the problem with metaphysics is that it is not useful. It does not contribute to technological advance. Thus, the primary purpose of scientific inquiry, in the era of embryonic positivism, was the generation of empirically proven knowledge with a social utility—not the development of rationally derived networks of knowledge statements.

Logical positivists interpret matters somewhat differently. Knowledge (and truth) is treated as a kind of idealized form of understanding. The characterization of *useful* knowledge versus *useless* metaphysics is replaced with the ideal of *true* knowledge versus *false* metaphysics. Embryonic positivism had lampooned and marginalized other forms of knowledge. Logical positivists take this a step further. Their mission is to stamp out the final vestiges of false (metaphysical) prophets—to convert the heathens and to ultimately subsume all fields of study to their rational truth. Reason, and reason alone, rules.

(3) The third premise of logical positivism strives to unify the various methods of inquiry across all branches of science. There is a single process to follow in all of the sciences. As noted earlier, any greater advances in the physical sciences, compared to the social sciences, are merely attributable to the greater maturity of the former. The certain (and inevitable) future shape of the social sciences can be seen in the laboratories and mathematical formulae of the physical sciences.

There are two related implications of this characterization of scientific inquiry. First, it follows that all scientific knowledge is ultimately reducible to a finite number of axiomatic statements. Granted, as a practical matter, it may not actually be possible to isolate a manageable number of foundational axiomatic statements. Nonetheless, scientific inquiry must be structured in a manner such that this is the goal or expectation. Thus the least developed social sciences, such as sociology, must imitate the methods and the language of the most advanced physical sciences, such as physics.

Scientific inquiry in the field of sociology must become a search for the laws governing the "physics" of social interaction. To be valid, all sociological knowledge must be articulated in the form of statements that can be experimentally tested.

A further related implication of this premise is that the pursuit of knowledge is not concerned with historical factors, because the categories and methods of science are universal. Scientific inquiry is blissfully ahistorical. To the extent that historical contingencies are allowed to affect a scientific result, the universal claims of science will be limited. Racism, as a social phenomenon, can be manifested in a variety of different forms over time (slavery, Jim Crow, the affirmative action backlash, etc.). However, the phenomenon of racism itself, in its most fundamental form, represents a universal human trait (a form of attribute-based hatred). Its historical origins are irrelevant. To try to understand the historically specific characteristics of racism is to overlook racism's general characteristics. It is the study of such general characteristics that will lead to insights regarding the link between a given social phenomenon (racism) and the universal laws governing human society. This focus alone will allow sociology to one day ascend the ladder of true scientific inquiry and join the hallowed pantheon of physical sciences.

(4) The fourth premise of logical positivism is the claim that the primary criterion for all meaningful knowledge is the verification principle. As discussed above, a statement is only considered meaningful if it is stated in a form that can be verified. Such statements lend themselves to the development of testable hypotheses—in other words, the verification of their content. This is the standard by which logical positivists determine whether to admit a statement into the language of scientific inquiry.

An unfortunate implication of the fourth premise is the difficulty of reconciling it with the first premise—that all statements must be either empirical or rational in form. Upon closer scrutiny it is evident that the verification principle itself does not meet this standard. Thus, on the basis of the verification principle, the following statement would not be considered meaningful.

The criterion for judging the meaningfulness of a statement is the verification principle.

The statement is not a rational claim with any empirical content. Furthermore, insofar as this statement represents the starting point for logical positivism—and given the rules of language adopted by the Vienna Circle—one must conclude that logical positivism is itself founded upon a metaphysical statement.

Logical positivists have responded that the verification principle is not a conditional rule in the logical sense. Rather, it is merely a definition of what constitutes a meaningful statement. However, this merely begs the question and one is left wondering why this definition and not another should be accepted. A further implication of this discrepancy—a rather unsettling one for logical positivism—is that logical positivism itself is a product of specific (and distinctly nonuniversal) cultural and historical factors. It has been suggested, therefore, that the metaphysical origins of the verification principle expose the underlying ideological nature of logical positivism, as well as its later variations. It is argued that logical positivism is squarely grounded in the historical and cultural values of its proponents rather than the neutral ether of a proclaimed pure objectivity. It was developed in a cultural age (early-twentieth-century Western Europe) that valued the advance of technological efficiency above all. It is this value, critics claim, rather than unadulterated reason, that ultimately shaped logical positivism.

(5) The fifth premise of logical positivism revolves around the movement from phenomenalism to physicalism and the reliance on intersubjective observation over individual observation. Through their marriage to physicalism, logical positivists now argued that empirical statements refer to social phenomena in a shared environment that can be commonly experienced. There must be intersubjective agreement among a community of observers that a statement accurately depicts a given phenomenon. Any observation or finding by a lone scientist must be replicable within a community of scientists. A scientific finding's truth depends upon its replicability.

The stunning and deflating implication of this premise is clear. Here is the final and irrevocable break from the search for an absolute and certain standard of knowledge. This is a search that is linked to an empirical tradition stretching back centuries. At last, for Bacon, Locke, Hume, and others, there is closure. Just as community standards determine what is filth and what is art, so too do community standards determine what is true and what is false. The age-old search for individual-based objectivity ends in communal subjectivity. The fact that community standards may change from time to time results in the rather troubling—though inevitable—conclusion that what is true and what is false will likewise alter over time and across societies.

FURTHER READING

Bechtel, William. "Logical Positivism: The Received View in Philosophy of Science." Pp. 17–50 in *Philosophy of Science*. Hillsdale, N.J.: Lawrence Erlbaum Associates, 1988.

Copleston, Frederick. "Some Reflections on Logical Positivism." Pp. 26–45 in *Contemporary Philosophy: Studies in Logical Positivism and Existentialism*. London: Burnes and Oates, 1965.

Halfpenny, Peter. "Logical Positivism." Pp. 46–62 in *Positivism and Sociology*. London: George Allen and Unwin, 1982.

Kolakowski, Leszek. "Logical Empiricism: A Scientific Defense of Threatened Civilization." Pp. 169–200 in *The Alienation of Reason: A History of Positivist Thought*. Garden City, N.J.: Doubleday, 1969.

Polkinghorne, Donald. "The Received View of Science." Pp. 59–93 in *Methodology for the Human Sciences*. Albany: SUNY Press, 1983.

3

Postpositivism

WHAT IS POSTPOSITIVISM?

The era of postpositivism brings our history of positivism up to the present day. Rather than leading to an idyllic, storybook finish, however, the final footpath along positivism's journey ultimately spirals off somewhat chaotically in a myriad of directions. For this reason, it is helpful to organize the discussion of postpositivism around three distinct groups. The first group—referred to here as the *late logical positivists*—consists of a committed cadre of thinkers in the 1940s and 1950s who attempted to resolve some of the brewing contradictions within logical positivism. In contrast to the earlier logical positivists, whose primary focus had been the physical sciences, the late logical positivists extended their analysis to historical and social explanations. Harking back to the nineteenth-century aspirations of Comte and Mill, they labored to apply the lawlike nature of deductive reasoning within the physical sciences to the social sciences. Much effort went toward devising sound procedures for testing and confirming a theory in the social sciences. Over time it became evident that the standards demanded by the logical positivists for a precise and exact language of scientific inquiry were more an ideal than a realistic goal. The goal, in turn, shifted. Discovering approximate truth, rather than absolute truth, was now the task of scientific inquiry.

The postpositivists are divided into two further groups. The *critical pessimists* consist of a curious blend of philosophers and social scientists who, beginning in the late 1950s, developed a critique of logical positivism that served as a vehicle to launch off in new research directions. By and large, the critical pessimists were content to watch gleefully as the positivist tradition smoldered in the rearview mirror. The *critical optimists* also developed a critique of logical positivism. Their approach, however, focused on the limitations of logical positivism, while attempting to retain the larger project of logical positivism in modified form. Both the pessimists and the optimists share a common concern for the, at times, wild contortions that were required of the late logical positivists to remain true to the programmatic ideals of logical positivism. Both pessimists and optimists argue that this is not so much a failure of human reason to construct proper measures that meet the demands of logical positivism as evidence of fundamental flaws within the underlying premises of logical positivism itself.

The current era of postpositivism is marked by two tendencies. On the one hand, there are the pessimists who seek to bury the positivist tradition. On the other hand, there are the optimists who seek to redeem positivism. For this reason, postpositivism does not bequeath a single legacy. In this respect, it is important to note that the late logical positivists—with crucial input from the critical optimists—represent the predominant tendency within standard research methods in the social sciences today.

WHAT ARE THE ORIGINS OF POSTPOSITIVISM?

Both tendencies within postpositivism—the pessimists and the optimists—trace their origins to a common critique of logical positivism that surfaced initially within the Vienna Circle. This critique has been closely associated with those who sought to preserve and extend the positivist tradition, the late logical positivists. This largely includes persons with direct ties to the Vienna Circle, such as Rudolf Carnap (1891–1970), Carl Hempel (1905–1997), Ernst Nagel (1901–1985), Richard Braithwaite (1900–1990), Hans Reichenbach (1891–1953), and Karl Popper (1902–1994).

Along with a large selection of specialized, polemical essays, the major works from the logical positivists include Popper's *Logic of Scientific Discovery* (1934), Reichenbach's *Experience and Prediction* (1938) and *The Rise of Scientific Philosophy* (1951), Hempel's *Fundamentals of Concept Formation in the Empirical Sciences* (1952),

Braithwaite's *Scientific Explanation: A Study of the Function of Theory, Probability, and Law in Science* (1955), and Nagel's *Structure of Science* (1961). This discussion of the late logical positivists' contributions to the origins of postpositivism is organized around four principal themes: (1) deductive-nomological arguments, (2) the characteristics of a law, (3) the confirmation of a law, and (4) causation.

Deductive-Nomological Arguments

In 1948, Carl Hempel and Paul Oppenheim (1885–1977) published a highly influential article that spawned an extended debate throughout the 1950s and 1960s. Briefly stated, Hempel and Oppenheim argue that within the social sciences (including the discipline of history) the proper method of deriving knowledge is the deductive-nomological approach. As one might gather from the name, the deductive-nomological model contains two basic elements. On the one hand, it is deductive. Thus, all claims (or theories) within the social sciences require a set of premises that implies a conclusion. On the other hand, it is nomological. Thus, all claims (and theories) within the social sciences must be based on general laws about society. Such laws are referred to as covering laws.

The following is an example of the deductive-nomological model.

> *All people, by nature, pursue their self-interest. It is in a person's self-interest to pursue leisure over work. Therefore, if you create disincentives for work (such as a generous welfare system), people will choose welfare over work. Likewise, if you create incentives for work (such as a minimal welfare system), people will choose work over welfare.*

In this case, the covering law is that human nature is such that people pursue their own self-interest. The premise is that, all things being equal, choosing leisure over work is consistent with pursuing one's self-interest. The conclusion that follows from this is that if there are incentives to accept welfare, people will not work. If there are disincentives to accept welfare, people will work. This covering law, in fact, is at the core of a vigorous public policy debate in the United States regarding the social impact of public assistance.

The basic deductive-nomological structure, as a foundation for scientific inquiry, was not a particularly novel concept for the physical sciences. However, the manner in which Hempel and Oppenheim apply this model to the social sciences raises fundamental issues. It is argued that many explanations within the social sciences—such as functionalist or historical explanations of events—either lack general laws altogether or, more often, they are incomplete. An incomplete explanation contains a set of premises that implies a conclusion. However, the set of premises is insufficient to reach the conclusion. The chief defect of incomplete arguments is that they do not allow predictions. Within scientific inquiry, prediction is as important as explanation, insofar as this is the only way to properly test a theory. It is only when all events are subsumed by general laws with a complete set of premises that both explanation and prediction are possible within a social theory.

The late logical positivists argued that the importance of the deductive-nomological approach lies in the fact that scientific inquiry is not simply the accumulation of conclusions but concerns the establishment of logically connected statements that argue for certain conclusions. Adherence to the deductive-nomological model allows others to reconstruct the reasoning process of a researcher after that researcher has justified his or her conclusions. This ensures that all the necessary premises for a conclusion are included. Scientific inquiry, in essence, is a process of systematic argumentation. This involves the development of complex networks of inferences between statements, few of which are actual direct observations. For this reason, an argument must be understood as a whole. Individual statements, in and of themselves, are irrelevant outside of the context in which they support the conclusion of a specific argument. This, of course, follows from Russell's earlier claim that the form of an argument, and not the truth of its statements, determines its validity.

The Characteristics of a Law

Laws are the foundation both for the deductive-nomological model and for the construction of theories. A theory is simply a system of deductively related laws. The goal of scientific inquiry is to create unified networks of laws (or theories). All laws share one basic trait: They make universal claims regarding observed regularities that apply at all times in all places. A law, therefore, is distinguishable from a singular statement of fact that is specific to time and place. This points to an important distinction between universal laws and accidental occurrences. Consider the following statements.

> *Statement 1.* Yesterday, while sitting on my porch, I saw a flock of birds flying south.
> *Statement 2.* Every fall flocks of birds fly south.

Statement 1 is a specific claim with a unique time and place, though it describes a common phenomenon. Statement 2 is a universal claim, though it could also be rephrased in the form of a specific statement like statement 1. All universal statements begin as specific statements. Over time, observed regularities suggest consistent patterns. These consistent patterns are then described as laws. Thus, laws are derived from direct observation; however, a law itself cannot be observed as such. There is therefore an inductive quality to the establishment of laws. For this reason, a law can never be developed with absolute certainty.

The standard form of a lawlike statement is referred to as the universal conditional. The standard version of this is: If A then B. This implies that, under all circumstances, if (A) I drop a bowling ball on my bare foot, then (B) I will be in pain. The statement is universal because it applies under all circumstances. The statement is also conditional because it gives the specific circumstances when I will feel pain. However, not all universal conditionals constitute laws. Consider the following statement: *All of the students in my class on February 22, 2002, arrived on time.* This statement appears to have the form of a universal conditional. However, it does not establish the general law that: *If I have students in my class, then they arrived on time.* This is because the events of February 22 represent an accidental occurrence that is specific to a place and time. Therefore, not all universal conditionals are laws. They must satisfy further criteria. Here, the late logical positivists turned to the role of counterfactuals. A counterfactual is a device for testing a universal conditional. It argues that, even though a certain event has not taken place, if it had, certain events would have followed. Compare the following example with the previous one.

All male students must wear ties at my all-male college where rules are never broken. Therefore, if I had given a class yesterday with twenty students, there would have been twenty students wearing ties in my class.

In the previous example, pertaining to students arriving in class on time, the counterfactual criterion cannot be applied. Given the universal conditional, as presented, there is no way to guarantee the claim that all of the students would have arrived on time if I had taught the class yesterday. (I could change the claim to satisfy the counterfactual criterion by adding the further condition that no one is admitted late to class in my school.) In the second example, pertaining to students wearing ties, the counterfactual criterion can be applied. Given the universal conditional, as presented, it is not possible for a student to have attended my class without a tie. So if twenty students went to class, there must have been twenty students wearing ties. As is evident from this formulation, the counterfactual criterion is as applicable to events from the past as to those in the future. In the case of past occurrences, when a universal conditional satisfies the counterfactual criterion, this is a lawlike *explanation*. In the case of future occurrences, when a universal conditional satisfies the counterfactual criterion, this represents a lawlike *prediction*.

The case of the all-male college where rules are never broken brings up a second point. Carnap notes that certain laws might meet the counterfactual criterion but only during a specific time period. In other words, the college rule regarding ties might change. If this were the case, then the example from above would need to be altered in the following fashion.

Between 1982 and 1989, all male students had to wear ties at my all-male college where rules are never broken. Therefore, if I had given a class on a date between 1982 and 1989 with twenty students, there would have been twenty students wearing ties in my class.

Carnap, in this respect, draws a further distinction between types of laws beyond the universal (those that are able to meet the counterfactual and are thus applicable in all times and places) and the accidental (those that are unable to meet the counterfactual criterion). In addition, there are basic laws and practical laws. Basic laws are universal laws that meet the counterfactual criterion. Practical laws are neither universal nor accidental. The example pertaining to students wearing ties between 1982 and 1989 is a case in point. Practical laws are often referred to as empirical generalizations rather than laws. This distinction follows from the fact that practical laws cannot form the bases for general theories. They are limited to providing descriptions of general tendencies that hold true under certain historically circumscribed conditions.

Empirical generalizations are similar to the provisional hypotheses based on observed regular patterns of occurrences that are associated with the inductive method. Many of the late logical positivists believed that such generalizations could serve a useful purpose within scientific inquiry. In an attempt to capture the developmental potential of empirical generalizations, Nagel refers to them as "experimental laws." As such, they can be formulated independently of an explicit theory. Because they are not deduced from theories, they are independent of theoretical implications. At the same time, precisely because experimental laws are based on empirical data—and not reducible to a theory—they can survive the defeat of any theory that others might attempt to associate with them. B. F. Skinner (1904–1990), for example, rejects theory building altogether in the social sciences, favoring the use of so-called descriptive behaviorism. Descriptive behaviorism limits scientific findings to the development of summary statements reporting correlations between observable variables.

The Confirmation of a Law

In the previous discussion much was said about the different characteristics of laws, while nothing was said about establishing the truth of laws. This is the role of confirmation. Efforts to better analyze the confirmation of laws followed from growing dissatisfaction with the verification principle. Upon further consideration, it became clear that the verification principle was really just an extension of the inductive method developed by Mill in the previous century. The inductive nature of the verification principle ultimately forced logical positivists to rely upon conclusions based on probability rather then certainty.

Karl Popper led the charge to minimize the inductive influence and to reground scientific inquiry in deductively connected statements linked to laws. It was argued that laws cannot be verified simply through the accumulation of evidence. Indeed, simply collecting further evidence could only *disprove* a law. Popper proposed resurrecting the hypothetical-deductive model with a modified emphasis. The hypothetical-deductive method relies upon a network of deductive inferences (hypotheses) to propose evidence statements (in the form of laws). In form, the hypothetical-deductive model is similar to the deductive-nomological model. To borrow from a previous example:

> *All people, by nature, pursue their self-interest. It is in a person's self-interest to pursue leisure over work. Therefore, if you create disincentives for work (such as a generous welfare system), people will choose welfare over work.*

The advantage of the hypothetic-deductive method is that it results in the development of laws that can be tested. Predictable observations can be deduced from the law. If a given prediction is contradicted, it can be safely concluded that the law is proven false. In the above example, were one to create disincentives for work through a generous welfare system and this did not lead people to choose welfare over work, then this would call into question either the premise, the law, or both. In Popper's hands, the hypothetical-deductive method, therefore, effectively inverts the verification principle. Rather than searching for evidence to verify a law, the purpose of scientific inquiry is to search for evidence to falsify a law. Certainty is only possible when a law is falsified. This is referred to as the principle of falsifiability. Thus, the hypothetical-deductive method—based on experimentation and collection of empirical data—can only falsify with certainty or verify with a high degree of probability. This again is because verification is a matter of inductive logic.

Causation

As briefly touched on in chapter 1, the notion of causation has always presented certain challenges for the positivist tradition. Hume and other empiricists dismissed the notion of causation as pure metaphysics. However, if a central purpose of scientific inquiry is to make predictions, than accounting for causation is no minor matter. The challenge for the late logical positivists, in this regard, is holding together the rocky marriage of rationalism and empiricism. The rationalist side of positivism emphasizes the role of deductive logic. Accordingly, all explanations are based on demonstrating that a specific event is the product of a general law. The empiricist side of positivism emphasizes the role of empirical observations (and deductions therefrom). Accordingly, all explanations are based on observable phenomena.

The dilemma regarding causation arises from the empiricist side, which holds that all knowledge is limited to empirical observations and deductions drawn from such observations. Causation is not an observable phenomenon. The best one can do is to claim that it has been the experience that event A and event B are somehow linked. Technically speaking, however, one cannot claim that they have observed that event A *produced* event B. To account for this, laws are characterized as mere descriptions of invariable associations between events. One type of invariable association—that associated with the notion of causation—is invariable sequence. Invariable sequence describes an ordered pattern of occurrence that defines the relationship between two events. A person dying after being shot in the heart is an example of an invariable sequence. Late logical positivists argue that it is necessary to replace the notion that one event produces another with the notion that a certain relationship (a form of invariable sequence) holds between two events.

This relationship is further specified as necessary and/or sufficient. If a necessary relationship exists between two events, then one cannot occur without the other. Oxygen and fire is an example of such a relationship. For fire to burn (event B), it is necessary for oxygen to be present (event A). In the second case, if a sufficient relationship exists between two events, then event B will always occur if event A occurs. However, event B might occur even when event A does not occur. For example, it is always the case that a person will die (event B) if she is deprived of oxygen (event A). However, a person will also die (event B) if she is shot in the heart—even if she is *not* deprived of oxygen (event A). Within the social sciences, it is most often the case that so-called causal arguments are, in fact, based on sufficient (and not necessary) relationships.

WHAT ARE THE MAIN ELEMENTS OF POSTPOSITIVISM?

Following the contributions of the late logical positivists, postpositivism emerged as a critique of logical positivism. This critique resulted in two tendencies—critical pessimism and critical optimism. Curiously enough, Ludwig Wittgenstein, whose *Tractatus* in 1922 had provided the galvanizing spark for logical positivism, was also a central figure contributing to its upheaval. Wittgenstein's *Philosophical Investigations* (1953) served as the impetus for the development of both the critical pessimists and the critical optimists. There is basic agreement among pessimists and optimists regarding many aspects of the general critique of logical positivism. They disagree, however, over what conclusions to draw from this critique.

Critical pessimists prefer to toss logical positivism overboard, along with the entire positivist tradition. Critical optimists are committed to radically reframing logical positivism in an effort to save the positivist tradition. The presentation of these two tendencies within postpositivism is organized around six central themes. These include (1) the later Wittgenstein and language games, (2) the pessimists' indictment of theory-laden observations, (3) the pessimists' emphasis on social context and the slide into relativism, (4) the optimists' accusations of fundamentalism among the pessimists, (5) the optimists' appeal to multiple patterns of reasoning, and (6) the controversy over a linear versus a disjointed history of scientific advances.

The Later Wittgenstein and Language Games

Between 1936 and 1951, Wittgenstein filled several volumes of personal notebooks that were never published in his lifetime. These works, published posthumously as *Philosophical Investigations*, marked a significant departure from his earlier views and signaled a major turning point in the life of positivism. The basic assumption of Wittgenstein's earlier work, *Tractatus* (and of logical positivism in general), was that it is possible to construct a formal language that describes reality as it truly is in a pure, unfiltered form. It was believed that words could directly name the phenomena that we observe and experience. This is the basis for protocol sentences. In

Philosophical Investigations, Wittgenstein calls into question this fundamental belief. He argues that it is not possible to postulate a direct relationship between a given phenomenon and a specific word. Rather, a word's meaning is determined by the circumstances in which it is used. Context determines meaning. With this minor revision, all hell broke loose.

By denying the possibility of universal meaning within language, Wittgenstein extinguished any hope for logical positivism, given its core assumptions. It was not ultimately possible to construct a universal descriptive language based on pure experience. The basic insights of *Philosophical Investigations* emerge from the notion of language games. A language game is any set of agreed-upon rules for communication and interaction. For instance, a southern dialect is a language game. If you are familiar with the style of speech in parts of the U.S. South, then specific words and phrases will have meaning to you. The rules of a spoken language are also referred to as grammar. However, language games do not always concern spoken languages. The sport of basketball constitutes a language game. If you are familiar with the rules of basketball, then you will understand how to participate in the sport. Outside of these very precise contexts, however, a phrase from a southern dialect or a strategy in basketball cannot be understood. Because of his emphasis on language and communication, the later Wittgenstein's influence is often referred to as the linguistic turn.

Three insights follow from this notion of language games and meaning. First, it is clear that anyone with a perspective outside a specific language game will be unable to interpret the meaning associated with words and actions of those who use the language game. There is no point outside a given language game from which to judge the language game. Imagine you were completely unfamiliar with the rules of basketball. In this case it would be impossible to judge a coach's defensive strategy. If you are positioned outside of basketball (as a language game), then it is impossible to interpret the meaning of such actions. Therefore, all criticisms (or interpretations) must be internal criticisms that emerge from within the language game. The task of social science is limited to determining which arguments are true within the limits of a given language game. Thus, any notion of the unity of sciences is pure illusion. Unity between two language games is nonsensical. It would be the equivalent of a baseball fan judging a basketball player by how many home runs he or she hit.

Second, the essential project of logical positivists—defining rules and standards for the use of words to represent reality—can only take place in a social context. This is because the use and development of a language game is an inherently social activity. Rules and standards are established by communities and cannot be developed by individuals. The purpose of a language game is to communicate thoughts and ideas among community members. It serves no purpose unless two or more persons are attempting to interact. This reflects the fact that words do not refer to objects in the world with preformed, essential meanings equally applicable in all social contexts. All meaning is socially defined and community specific.

Third, because all meaning is determined by the specific rules of different language games, all statements depicting observations are, by definition, theory laden. To say that a statement is "theory laden" is simply to argue that (1) its meaning is dependent on the rules of a specific language game and (2) it does not necessarily have meaning outside that language game. Wittgenstein emphasizes the role of theories because, within the hypothetic-deductive method, the purpose of scientific inquiry is to test theoretical claims. Thus, it is argued that all observation statements reflect preconceived notions of the world that are based in the specific language game from which the theoretical claims originated. It follows that all observation is theory laden.

The perspective that emerged from *Philosophical Investigations* was fairly devastating for the agenda of logical positivism. If all knowledge is relative to one's unique perspective, then, ultimately, the pursuit of truth is without basis. Neither pure sense data nor formal logic offers an absolute foundation for knowledge. All sense data and all applications of logic are products of historically and culturally specific language games. Last, it is worth noting that these ideas of Wittgenstein regarding language games were not entirely new. Ferdinand de Saussure (1857–1913), among others, had developed similar interpretations decades earlier. (This is discussed in the context of structuralism and linguistics in chapter 4.) The influence of *Philosophical Investigations* was, therefore, as much a function of Wittgenstein's notoriety among members of the Vienna Circle as it was of the originality of his thoughts.

The Theory-Laden Nature of Observations

Wittgenstein was hardly alone in his concern for the theory-laden nature of observations. Among those contributing to this debate are Willard Quine, *From a Logical Point of View* (1953), *Word and Object* (1964); Mary Hesse, *The Structure of Scientific Inference* (1974); and Peter Achinstein, *Concepts of Science* (1968). While acknowledging their intellectual debt to the ideas of Wittgenstein, many participants in the debate—especially Quine and Hesse—also draw inspiration from the earlier work of Pierre Duhem (1861–1916), *Aim and Structure of Physical Theory* (1906). The theory-laden nature of observation implies that, within scientific inquiry, it is impossible to carry out observations that are uncontaminated by theory. Simply put, observation requires classification. Classification schemes presuppose theoretical models of reality. Thus, within scientific inquiry, the character of observations is determined by theory. Consider the following example:

> You are conducting research in which you pretend to be a homeless person asking for money on the street to test the theory that certain types of people will be friendlier than others. You have been asked to characterize the nature of responses as friendly, unfriendly, or indifferent. As you interact with people, you must conform your observations in a manner that allows you to narrow and classify their broad range of responses into one of three categories. In this manner you filter out a host of further potential observations. Your observations conform to your preset categories, which are theory based.

Observation and experience is the process of cataloging and categorizing phenomena according to preset concepts. Experience, therefore, represents a staged interaction between one's established conceptual framework and the environment. In turn, established conceptual frameworks originate in the dominant beliefs of one's community. At one level, this is not too different from Richard Avenarius's notion of apperceptive masses discussed in chapter 2. It will be recalled that, according to Avenarius, as we navigate our environment we rely upon a store of past experiences (apperceptive masses) to interpret and categorize that which we encounter. The basic difference between Avenarius and the critical pessimists is that Avenarius contends that there are standards for judging one community's views about reality against another community's views. Scientific researchers, for example, can be trained in a manner that endows them with the capacity (the proper apperceptive masses) to identify and categorize scientific phenomena more accurately than others. The pessimists questioned the certainty with which one community's criteria could be said to be more accurate than another's.

A further important consequence of the theory-laden nature of observation concerns the difficulty of definitively disproving a hypothesis through observation—as Popper endeavored to do through the principle of falsification. Generally speaking, observations are not linked to just one theoretical statement. In fact, they are connected to a whole system of theories and assumptions. For this reason, a specific, lawlike statement cannot be judged in isolation from an entire network of statements. Thus, the fact that an observation happens to contradict the deductive logic of a given hypothesis does not necessarily refute the covering law from which the hypothesis was derived. Rather, it might be possible to make adjustments within the larger network of statements—including how measurements are taken—so that the covering law can be vindicated. For example:

> *Covering law:* In U.S. society, whites will not live in the same neighborhood with significant numbers of African Americans.
> *Hypothesis:* A significant number of African Americans (20 percent or more of the population) moving to an all-white neighborhood will cause whites to move.
> *Observation refuting hypothesis:* Over a five-year period, the all-white neighborhood of Shangri-La became 25 percent African American and no whites moved out.

At this point there are two choices. You can declare your covering law to be refuted, or you can revisit the assumptions built into your hypothesis. If your faith in the covering law remains unshaken, then you must look to revise your hypothesis. Perhaps the hypothesis requires ten years, not five, to pass. Perhaps, the definition of "significant numbers" of African Americans (20 percent or more of the families) must be raised to 30 percent. Or perhaps there were measurement errors and you need to redefine the boundaries of the neighborhood. The point here is that the hypothesis derived from the covering law contains many assumptions not directly dependent upon the truth of the covering law. Should an observation contradict a hypothesis based on the covering law, then the hypothesis (or a number of its assumptions) can be reformulated without affecting the covering law. This points to the inherent danger of the theory-laden nature of observations. They permit one to structure scientific inquiry in a manner that prejudices the results—consciously or subconsciously.

Social Context and Relativism

It follows from the previous discussion that the interpretation and meaning of social phenomena are determined by social context. The exact same phenomenon can have completely opposite meanings in two different social contexts. The danger of attributing meaning to social context in this manner is that it tends to lead to complete relativism. This issue was discussed by many, including Benjamin Whorf (1897–1941), *Language, Thought, and Reality* (1956); Peter Winch (1926–), *The Idea of a Social Science and Its Relation to Philosophy* (1958); Michael Polanyi (1891–1976), *Personal Knowledge* (1958); Norwood Hanson (1924–1967), *Patterns of Discovery* (1968); and Paul Feyerabend (1924–1994), *Against Method* (1975). Peter Winch was one of the first to attempt to apply Wittgenstein's insights regarding language games to the social sciences. While Wittgenstein had focused on the use of spoken languages, Winch expanded the role of language games to other forms of social interaction.

In this regard, the nature of social action is key. Winch defines social action as collective behavior within a system of meaning and symbolism. It is helpful here to distinguish between "social action" and "human behavior." Social action implies activity that has meaning only when it is validated and reciprocated in a social context. Human behavior implies activity with individual subjective meaning. Consider a student in a classroom who raises his or her hand to be recognized by the instructor. On the one hand, the act of raising one's hand is a social action. In the given social context, the student is using a symbolic gesture that is understood to indicate the desire to speak. On the other hand, the act of raising one's hand is a human behavior. It reflects a judgment at the level of the student's individual subjectivity that there is something he or she would like to say.

Social action is, therefore, a purposeful activity carried out within a specific set of rules and standards. It has meaning only within the context of a specific language game and has no meaning when analyzed as an individual act severed from its social milieu. Such acts require little or no deliberate reflection on the part of persons who share the language game. Upon leaving a room, one can generally wave good-bye without fear that this gesture will be mistaken for a threat or for an attempt to hail a cab. Persons operating within the same language game are able to rely upon a host of implicit signs and gestures to communicate a variety of thoughts, ideas, and feelings without explicit commentary.

Understanding social action implies understanding the social meaning that is embedded in action. To accurately portray the activities of a particular culture or social context, a social scientist must, therefore, first ensure an accurate understanding of the language game of local participants. Indeed, Winch and others strenuously argue that there is an inherent conflict in efforts to analyze cultures other than one's own. This follows from the researcher's reliance on categories of analysis that originate in his or her own culture (or language game) and not in the subjects'. It is not possible to meaningfully apply categories of explanation that were developed for one social context (or language game) in another social context. At best one will generate a distorted image of the other social context. At worst, one will produce pure ideology.

Imagine you want to understand the dominant family structure in an unfamiliar society. You enter the culture with a preset notion of what constitutes a family—its characteristics, functions, roles, etc. To the extent that you impose these preset notions on the culture that you enter, you will distort the subjects' reality to fit yours. Suppose that one of your preset notions is that a family is a subunit of a society that raises a set of children linked by birth relationships. This may or may not conform to the local reality. However, if your starting point is to discover how subunits clustered around mothers raise children, then it is quite likely that you will, in fact, be able to construct some variation of this form. Similarly, one can envision a researcher from a society in which the dominant family structure emphasizes community-level child rearing, rather than subunits. Were such a researcher to study the United States, she too—after some effort—could construct variations conforming to her preset notions.

Those emphasizing the relationship between social context and social meaning place a particular stress on how rules of reasoning are themselves products of a local culture's language game. Therefore, consistent with Wittgenstein, value judgments simply ape the norms and beliefs of a given cultural setting, rather than representing universal, transcendent truths. For example:

> *Event:* A doctor administers medicine to an ill boy and he is subsequently restored to health. *Explanation 1:* One language game, employing a biomedical-based rationale, concludes that certain properties in the medicine have healed the boy. *Explanation 2:* Another language game, employing a spirit-based rationale, concludes that the doctor has acted in a manner that is pleasing to the spirits and this has healed the boy.

Within the rules and standards of the respective language game, each is correct. However, within the rules and standards of logical positivism—as a language game—one can only work with the rationale of one language game. For this reason, explanation 1 is declared to be modern and explanation 2 is viewed as primitive. The categories of modern and primitive can be confusing, however. For example, many Christians in the United States adopt a version of the primitive explanation above when they argue that the United States enjoys the status of the most powerful nation in the world today precisely because their God looks favorably upon the country.

Benjamin Whorf argued that the social world constitutes a linguistic construct. Each community's language shapes its members' perceptions of reality. When two communities' perceptions differ, neither can be said to be more accurate than the other. Rather, each community's perception is accurate insofar as it fits the community's language scheme. As might be expected, such views were soon attacked as promoting a hopeless relativism. There is no basis for comparing two cultures or for making judgments about different societies with reference to an objective viewpoint. If some Somali parents want to brutalize and mutilate their young daughters through female circumcision, then that is just their way of doing things. Who are we to judge? I. C. Jarvie's criticisms are typical in this regard. In *Revolution in Anthropology* (1964), Jarvie argues that, the basic cautions offered by Winch and Whorf aside, it is still possible to draw meaningful comparisons between distinct cultures and to offer constructive criticism from a vantage point outside a given language game.

The Optimists' Accusations of Fundamentalism

By the late 1960s, many of those working in the positivist tradition had had enough. A self-respecting positivist could take just so much. The wanton relativism and reckless speculation of critics of positivism had goaded the grandchildren of Comte into a fight. Among those leading the charge were Gerard Radnitzky, *Contemporary Schools of Metascience* (1968–1973); Imre Lakatos (with Alan Musgrave), *Criticism and the Growth of Knowledge* (1970); Dudley Shapere, *Philosophical Problems in Natural Science* (1965); Larry Laudan, *Progress and Its Problems: Toward a Theory of Scientific Growth* (1977); and Stephen Toulmin, *Human Understanding: The Collective Use and Evolution of Concepts* (1972). The optimists readily acknowledge the challenging critique of Wittgenstein and other pessimists. However, this recognition is combined with an uncompromising belief that, in the end, scientific inquiry can overcome such challenges and continue to make tangible and steady progress toward more accurate descriptions of reality.

At the heart of the optimists' case is the claim that both the logical positivists and the pessimists share the same mistaken belief—originating with interpretations of René Descartes (1596–1650)—that absolute certainty is the only standard of genuine knowledge. This suggests a latent fundamentalist streak running through the pessimists. Logical positivists believed that certainty is an aim of scientific inquiry and attempt to construct models of inquiry to achieve this. The pessimists detail the failures of logical positivists to achieve absolute certainty and determine, therefore, that there can be no single, unassailable standard of truth. The pessimists then conclude that all knowledge claims are equally valid within the context of the language game in which they are formulated. The optimists reject not only the the pessimists' responses to the failures of logical positivism but also the project of the logical positivists itself. Instead, Radnitzky and others opt for a so-called third way based on an explicit and critical recognition of the limits of human knowledge. Progress in human understanding is possible. However, knowledge claims about reality are never absolute and certain.

Multiple Patterns of Reasoning and Fallibilism

The optimists flatly reject the notion that scientific inquiry can only make knowledge claims within a specific language game. Rather, they argue that over time knowledge progresses and we are able to come closer and closer to describing reality as it really is. After all, as Comte pointed out a hundred years earlier, advanced Western society had itself gone through a period of mysticism when healing properties were attributed to magical spirits—as in the case of the "primitive" society described above. However, with advances in knowledge about the world, biomedical explanations replaced spirit-based explanations.

This is evidence that movement from one so-called language game to another is possible. Furthermore, it is evidence that, in fact, a single, universal criterion can be used to analyze two language games—in this case, the efficacy of healing techniques. Prior to the introduction of biomedicine, spirit-based healing was the only language game in the realm of medicine that people were familiar with. Nonetheless, using the criteria of their only known language game (spirit-based healing), they were able to rationally judge the value of an unfamiliar language game (biomedicine) and adopt it.

The optimists believe that part of the misunderstanding lies in the logical positivists' emphasis on the standard of absolute certainty and the role of deductive logic. In this way, the logical positivists had overlooked other methods of producing and testing knowledge claims. The optimists concur with those critics of logical positivism who argue that there are patterns of reasoning beyond basic deductive logic that guide scientific inquiry. For example, within scientific inquiry different patterns of reasoning are associated with the process of discovery (developing hypotheses) and the process of justification (testing hypotheses). At the same time, there are multiple patterns of reasoning even within the process of discovery and the process of justification.

In this regard, the optimists place a greater emphasis on the process of discovery than the logical positivists, whose emphasis had been the process of justification. Ironically, this is a distinction originally emphasized by a leading logical positivist, Hans Reichenbach, in *Experience and Prediction* (1938). Within the process of discovery, a wide variety of patterns of reasoning are employed to postulate hypotheses. However, even within the process of justification, deductive logic is merely one pattern of rationality. Nonetheless, the fact that scientific inquiry relies upon multiple patterns of reasoning does not imply that we lack sound bases for judging one pattern of reasoning more accurate or appropriate than another.

We are constantly maneuvering between multiple patterns of reasoning in our everyday lives. In the morning, a high school student may be asked to explain the process of photosynthesis in plant life. To do so, she will need to rely upon her familiarity with the reasoning pattern associated with the physical sciences. Later that afternoon, the same student may wrestle with the fact that she has too little money to buy all she wants. Here she will need to rely upon her familiarity with the reasoning pattern associated with rational choice and consumer behavior. That same evening, the student may learn of a distant relative's death and will share in the family's grieving. To do so she will need to rely upon her familiarity with the reasoning pattern associated with spiritual matters. In each case, the student is able to maneuver relatively easily between scenarios using a store of knowledge regarding which pattern of reasoning to employ in each situation.

Just as in our everyday lives, it is argued, scientific inquiry also offers multiple patterns of reasoning to solve various conceptual problems. Understood in this sense, "rationality" concerns all problem-solving activities. Rationality is not simply a subspecies of logic whereby the internal consistency of concepts and beliefs alone is the proper measure. Rather, the proper gauge of rationality is the process by which knowledge claims are modified in the face of contradictory findings. Scientific inquiry involves the ongoing development and improvement of its patterns of reasoning as it crashes into and overcomes the limits of its formulations. The optimists argue that what the logical positivists and pessimists fail to appreciate is that scientific inquiry is a historically evolving social activity that is constantly varying its pattern of reasoning and developing new rationales.

Popper, Radnitzky, and other optimists organize their notions concerning multiple patterns of reasoning around the concept of fallibilism. Fallibilism concerns the process of determining whether there are good reasons to consider one knowledge claim to be more accurate than another. This entails an important distinction between confirmation and rational decision making. Confirmation— the central concern of logical positivism—is merely a logical process that calculates the probability of truth. Rational decision making is that process within scientific inquiry in which rival knowledge claims are forced to answer to one another's criticisms, a subpart of which involves confirmation. The explicit and critical recognition of the limits of human knowledge is based on rational decision making. In the end, advances in scientific inquiry occur as researchers develop sound rationales for provisionally preferring one knowledge claim over another. This is done with the understanding that, in all likelihood, today's indisputable truth will be tomorrow's flat-earth theory.

Linear versus Nonlinear Progress

A rather disturbing consequence of the pessimists' critique of logical positivism is the possibility of nonlinear change. If each language game contains its own set of rules and standards, it follows that when a society moves from one language game to another— owing to conquest or internal crisis—the new language game will likely retain few if any remnants of the previous language game's rules and standards. The pessimists extend this scenario from the realm of social conflict to that of scientific inquiry. This is a position strongly challenged by the optimists.

In 1962, Thomas Kuhn set out to challenge certain standard assumptions within scientific inquiry (based on logical positivism) with his short book *The Structure of Scientific Revolutions*. Kuhn's thesis is that advances in scientific inquiry develop by means of disjointed and discontinuous leaps rather than through a process of orderly, evolutionary progress. All scientific inquiry occurs within a paradigm. A paradigm is a conceptual system containing basic assumptions of how the world operates. This is akin to—but not exactly the same as—a language game. Each paradigm contains its own logic and is not necessarily related to other paradigms. One paradigm does not emerge or evolve from another. Rather, a revolutionary switch in paradigms occurs when contradictions emerge within a given paradigm. The new paradigm does not necessarily retain elements of the previous paradigm after simply resolving certain contradictions. It is not necessarily built on an earlier foundation. Thus, the movement to a new paradigm is discontinuous and arational. There is no discernible pattern associated with the switch from one paradigm to another.

While highly influential, Kuhn's thesis was swiftly attacked by those who viewed scientific progress in a more linear fashion. Popper, in *Objective Knowledge: An Evolutionary Approach* (1979), as well as Toulmin, in *Human Understanding* (1972), argue that, in fact, advances in scientific inquiry proceed by means of evolutionary trial and error. Rival views and concepts, regardless of paradigm, are submitted to intense empirical testing and one is declared the winner. Reasoned and deliberative continuity, not rupture, is the norm when tracking advances in scientific inquiry.

WHAT ARE THE IMPLICATIONS OF POSTPOSITIVISM?

The implications of postpositivism have been far-reaching. They extend well beyond the laboratory of the physical sciences to the social sciences and to much of the humanities. The world born of embryonic positivism and perfected by logical positivism had attempted to furnish a universal crucible for truth and knowledge. Many in the social sciences eagerly imitated the logical positivists' efforts. The critique of postpositivism was, therefore, devastating not only for the physical sciences but also for other fields. Given the continued allegiance of critical optimists to the historic project of positivism, albeit in radically modified form, their critique is of particular interest. The critical optimists' perspective continues to exercise a strong influence on the predominant research approaches in the social sciences. The implications of postpositivism can be organized around four central premises.

(1) The first premise of postpositivism concerns the inherently relative nature of knowledge statements. Because absolute certainty is unobtainable, the pessimists insist that we are reduced to a hopeless relativism wherein there are no sound bases for judging one knowledge statement to be more accurate than another. If one group of people believes that modern medicine is the basis for

restoring health and another group attributes healing to spiritual powers, each belief may be equally true within the rules and standards of each group's language game. The optimists agree that any hunt for absolute certainty will prove fruitless. However, they do not concede that the only alternative is complete anarchy. Rather, there are valid reasons for selecting one position over another based on how well researchers argue their case and marshal their evidence.

The implication of the optimists' position is that postpositivist scientific inquiry must rely on a combination of sound arguments and credible, convincing evidence. A conclusion cannot be reached with absolute certainty. However, the validity of one conclusion can be judged against that of another on the basis of a common set of criteria, the internal consistency of each argument, and the weight of evidence supporting a conclusion. It is true that the accuracy of competing knowledge statements is relative. However, it is also the case that the truth of a statement is a measure of degrees of accuracy that can be judged against a common set of criteria. Scientific inquiry resembles systematic problem-solving activities that result in conclusions based on stronger or weaker arguments.

(2) The second premise of postpositivism asserts that even to the extent that a knowledge statement is true, it is only provisionally true. There is no basis for believing that any statement found to be true today will not be refuted tomorrow. This occurs not because of any change in the conditions making the statement true but because of a change in the framework within which we judge one statement against another. The first premise holds that all knowledge statements are relative. We cannot say with absolute certainty that one conclusion is more accurate than another. The second premise pushes uncertainty a step further. Not only the conclusion but also the very basis for judging one conclusion more accurate than another can change. The very foundation of truth is constantly shifting and our criteria for judgment are inherently unstable.

The implications of a constantly shifting foundation of truth are a bit trickier than the issue of relativism between knowledge statements. One must argue not only for the accuracy of a given knowledge statement within the rules and standards of a given language game but also for the validity of the rules and standards of the language game itself. A brief example will illustrate. Imagine two researchers discussing the causes of poverty. The first develops an argument and gathers evidence to demonstrate that poverty is the product of individual laziness. The second develops an argument and gathers evidence to demonstrate that poverty is the product of social conditions. The two argue vigorously and angrily until they grow agitated and storm off.

The two may strenuously disagree, but their disagreement is based on a shared language game. For instance, both agree that poverty exists, that it insults human dignity, and that it is a societal problem. Indeed, it is only because of these shared values from a common language game that each can become so upset. Now imagine someone from another language game, based on alternative rules and standards, entering the debate. From the perspective of this language game, poverty does not exist, is not related to human dignity, and is therefore not considered a social problem. There is no basis for dialogue in this case. The values and concepts are completely antithetical.

For the sake of argument, let's say that the person arguing that individual laziness is the cause of poverty had the stronger argument and that this belief came to dominate social attitudes. The argument is provisional in the sense that an alternative language game (with alternative rules and standards for judging poverty) might one day supplant the current one. Importantly, the argument is not provisional in the sense that someday the person arguing for social conditions might be proven more accurate. This may or may not occur, given that all knowledge statements are only relatively true. However, the notion that all knowledge statements are only relatively true is distinct from the notion that all knowledge statements are provisional.

Remember, despite the advances of non-Euclidean geometry, the rules and standards of Euclidean geometry remain true within the limits of Euclidean geometry (as a language game). However, while one was operating within the norms of Euclidean geometry, it was impossible to foresee the world that was opened up through non-Euclidean geometry. The knowledge statements based on Euclidean geometry offered a view of the world that was provisional. Likewise, because we lack the ability to see into the future, today all knowledge statements regarding the cause of poverty are considered provisional.

(3) The third premise of postpositivism concerns the social and cultural influences in knowledge production. The heart of this premise is that knowledge about the world, and one's understanding of society, is largely shaped by a person's social and cultural background. In other words, the knowledge statements we use to organize our world and the language games we rely on to communicate our thoughts are the products of our specific social and historical conditions. As a consequence, social and cultural values—rather than the pure pursuit of truth—shape scientific inquiry. These values determine what subjects are researched and how research findings are presented and used. At the same time, the fact that social and cultural values shape scientific inquiry is never acknowledged within the process. Rather, it is assumed that the dominant values driving scientific inquiry—such as the pure pursuit of truth—are universal values that benefit everyone in society and should be extended to other societies.

The implications of the social and cultural influences on knowledge production are troubling. Matters are difficult enough when the truth of a knowledge statement is merely relative to other knowledge statements (premise 1) or when the very basis for judging the truth of a knowledge statement turns out to be provisional, resting upon a constantly shifting foundation (premise 2). Now we learn, in addition, that a knowledge statement is actually a product of social and cultural values. These social and cultural values, in turn, represent various complementary and conflictual social interests. Thus, beyond analyzing an argument and its supporting evidence, one must also now factor in how certain social groups might benefit from its acceptance or rejection.

Just as observations may be theory laden, theories turn out to be interest laden. Certain social groups might benefit from a particular interpretation of poverty and they might harness their resources to build a case for this position. With greater resources, some social groups can construct better-researched arguments with more voluminous evidence. However, this may tell us more about resource distribution in society than about the merits of the actual argument. Ultimately, the influence of social and cultural values can allow class interests (or other social interests) to determine which knowledge statements are accepted and which are rejected.

(4) The fourth premise of postpositivism concerns the linear nature of knowledge production. It is critical to the optimists that

the development of knowledge proceed in a fashion promoting linear progress. This is one of the few legacies of the Enlightenment to which the critical optimists remain steadfast in their faith. The truth of one knowledge statement may be relative to that of another and a certain language game may only provisionally rule. This the optimists will concede. However, knowledge itself does progress over time, they insist. We know more things more accurately today than we did yesterday and we will know yet more tomorrow. The history of all fields of scientific inquiry demonstrates this principle. In this way, scientific inquiry is cumulative and linear. One knowledge statement defeating a weaker claim or one language game supplanting another is not a random or haphazard event. It marks a heroic moment in the long march of human progress.

The implications of linear knowledge production primarily concern the third premise regarding the cultural influences on knowledge production. The argument that knowledge is progressive implies that certain language games represent reality more accurately than others. Over time, this claim is tested and "modern" language games replace "primitive" ones. However, if social and cultural values also determine which language games predominate, then it is unclear how we are to determine whether the imposition of one society's language game on another society is based on greater reason or greater gunpowder. There is an implicit argument among those promoting linear progress that those ruling others (or those whose interests dominate within society) do so by virtue of greater reason. Furthermore, it follows that there are those who need to be brought more fully into the sweep of world history and enlightened by the evolutionary and continuous store of human truths. Today's euphoria about globalization is based upon the same rationale today as were the Crusades in an earlier era.

FURTHER READING

Giddens, Anthony. "Positivism and Its Critics." Pp. 237–287 in *A History of Sociological Analysis*. Edited by Tom Bottomore and Robert Nisbett. New York: Basic Books. 1978.

Hughes, John. "The Positivist Orthodoxy." Pp. 16–34 in *The Philosophy of Social Research*. 2nd ed. London: Longman, 1997.

Morrow, Raymond, and David Brown. "Postempiricist Critiques of Positivism and Empiricism." Pp. 62–81 in *Critical Theory and Methodology*. Thousand Oaks, Calif.: Sage, 1994.

Phillips, Denis. "Postpositivistic Science: Myths and Realities." Pp. 31–46 in *The Paradigm Dialog*. Edited by Egon Guba. Newbury Park, Calif.: Sage, 1990.

Phillips, Denis, and Nicholas Burbules. "Philosophical Commitments of Postpositivist Researchers." Pp. 29–45 in *Postpositivism and Educational Research*. Lanham, Md.: Rowman & Littlefield, 2000.

4

Structuralism

Structuralism presents a framework for understanding social phenomena based on a radical alteration of one's everyday perception of the social world. The immediate world around one is less important than the larger reality behind that world. The study of the social world from a structural perspective reveals certain organizational rules and patterns that give it a definite form and structure. This form and structure—often referred to as a system or a whole—is the proper subject of structural analysis. Specific social phenomena only have meaning and can only be understood by placing them in this broader context. It is not that social phenomena are dropped from the analysis; rather, they are viewed as constituent parts of complex systems (or wholes). Their meaning is determined by their organizational role within a complex system. Owing to this emphasis on the structure, in the form of a system, structuralism is often referred to as systems (or holistic) analysis.

Within this framework of analysis, social phenomena stand in relation to a system just as a part stands in relation to a whole. Any part (or social phenomenon) in isolation is meaningless. It is the network of relationships between parts—determined by the order and sets of rules governing the system—that bestows meaning on each part. The significance of a part is, therefore, defined by its relation to the whole. Consider the example of rural hunger as a social phenomenon. From the perspective of structuralism, the part in this scenario would be an individual family without enough food. The system is the network of socioeconomic conditions within which this family struggles to get food. This includes the local labor market, the transportation system, the family's social support network, and regional social services. To understand why this family is hungry, one cannot simply consider its unique characteristics. Rather, one must examine the complex system within which the family is embedded and explore how the structures within this system either facilitate or impair the family's ability to obtain food.

Systems are characterized by two further features. They are open and self-regulating. Systems are open in the sense that they interact with and are influenced by the environment outside the immediate system. Thus, systems are dynamic and can be highly flexible. Systems are self-regulating in the sense that they rely upon a set of internal mechanisms to sustain themselves. Structuralists argue that a system does not simply emerge by random chance. It serves a specific role and its constituent parts are designed to perpetuate this role. Each system is able to adapt to societal changes and reorganize its parts to meet changing needs. The child welfare system in the United States, for example, has evolved over the past century through a constant process of adaptation to changing political and socioeconomic demands.

Structuralism can, therefore, be thought of as an effort to understand and define the relationships between parts and wholes within systems. This chapter examines three specific forms of structural analysis. Each was highly influential in the period when structuralism was first formulating its basic principles within the social sciences. (1) Functionalism is a form of structural analysis based on the belief that the purpose of social analysis is to understand the specific role of certain social practices in maintaining social stability. Functionalism analyzes the specific manner by which social practices (e.g., a preference for male offspring) have social meaning in the context of perpetuating the social order. (2) Linguistics is a form of structural analysis based on the belief that there are universal structures embedded in human languages. Linguistic analysis entails a careful dissection of language as a complex system of symbols and signs with specific social meaning. Language is both a reflection and a product of complex social interaction. (3) Structural anthropology is a form of structural analysis based on the belief that there are universal structures across diverse cultural practices. Structural anthropology analyzes specific cultural practices (e.g., family life) as complex systems with shared social meaning across societies. It tries to extend the basic analysis of linguistics beyond language to a broad range of cultural practices.

Structuralism shares certain characteristics with the positivist tradition. For example, structuralists make use of the deductive-nomological model discussed in chapter 3. Indeed, in some ways, structuralism represents the deductive-nomological model on steroids. However, whereas positivists use observations to establish patterns and laws, structuralists tend to posit universal laws and then carry out observations to confirm these laws. This points to a central distinction between positivism and structuralism regarding how research is conducted. Positivists frame their analysis at the level of observable social phenomena. Structuralists frame their analysis at the level of theoretical systems (composed of social phenomena). To some extent, this is merely a difference of emphasis. However, as explored in this chapter, it also suggests fundamental differences over how best to investigate and understand the social world.

One general warning is in order at this point. The distinction that structuralists draw between parts and wholes leads to a certain degree of confusion between method and theory. This issue is also present in positivism and other methodological orientations, but the problem appears more acutely in structuralism. Put simply, it is a question of the extent to which structuralism represents a method—a description of the process by which we generate knowledge about social phenomena—and the extent to which it represents a theory—an explanation accounting for the nature of social phenomena. In depicting structuralism, the discussion may seem more theoretical than methodological. This follows, in part, from the contention of postpositivists that all observations are inherently theory laden. (See chapter 3.) In other words, a structuralist may make detailed observations of parts; however, this is only done after an analysis of the system has informed the researcher what to look for. Thus, it is difficult to treat method and theory separately. These issues are dealt with most explicitly in the section on implications in this chapter.

WHAT ARE THE ORIGINS OF STRUCTURALISM?

Structuralism emerged from three general traditions. (1) Within the physical sciences (in particular biology) there was a strong movement by the late nineteenth century to study organisms as complex organic structures. (2) Within one branch of the social sciences there was a similar push at the time to understand social structures (such as religious institutions) as complex systems. (3) Within a second branch of the social sciences there was an interest in understanding cognitive structures (such as language) as complex systems. The three developed as separate and distinct enterprises, yet each was influenced by the others. Auguste Comte, for example, played a pivotal role in recasting the biological model in a conceptual language that resulted in an interpretation of society as a social organism. Like the human body, Comte argued, society can be thought of as possessing parts and suborgans (or subsystems). Indeed, there were sharp parallels between developments in the fields of biology, sociology, and linguistics in the late nineteenth and early twentieth century.

One of the challenges in examining structuralism—due to its cross-disciplinary origins—is that separate disciplines often frame similar concepts slightly differently. For this reason, it is helpful to organize the discussion around three core subject areas. (1) Organic structures pertain to the physical world, particularly biology. (2) Social structures pertain to the social world of aggregated populations. (3) Cognitive structures pertain to how people use thought processes and language to interpret and communicate experience. Each core subject area deals with a distinct subject matter, yet each tends to freely borrow concepts and terminology from the others. This is good insofar as it creates a common field of study. However, it can also be confusing. At times, the same word or concept is used with different meanings. For this reason, it is essential to keep in mind the subject matter under discussion when considering debates within structuralism.

Organic Structures

The notion of organic structures as systems emerged from a basic dilemma in biology. In the initial period following the publication of Charles Darwin's (1809–1882) *On the Origin of Species by Means of Natural Selection* (1859) there was an inherent difficulty in explaining the concept of evolution through the traditional tools of deductive and inductive reasoning. Because the processes were so gradual, occurring over great stretches of time, they were impossible to observe. (The mechanism for such an explanation was not provided until the later development of Gregor Johann Mendel's [1822–1884] work in the field of genetics.) From this debate emerged the concept of organicism, which explained biological entities as complex organic systems interacting with their environment.

Henri Bergson (1859–1941) and Hans Driesch (1867–1941) were leading proponents of this perspective emphasizing organic structures. Their texts, Bergson's *Creative Evolution* (1907) and Driesch's *Science and Philosophy of the Organism* (1908), were central to the development of this work. They argued that there were "forces" within an organism (Driesch referred to this as entelechy) that somehow drove an organism toward its development. This force could not be understood simply by studying the organism's individual parts. According to Driesch, each organism contains this quality, which is described as a nonphysical agent that drives physiological developments in such a fashion as to assure that an organism always tends to return to a normal, steady state of equilibrium.

Within this formulation, the organic whole—as an organized entity—is understood to be a unique form that is distinguishable from its constituent parts. It is not merely a combination of parts. This is what is meant by the popular expression "The whole is greater than the sum of its parts." In other words, the organic whole is not simply the sum of a collection of independent parts. Rather, the manner in which the parts are interconnected constitutes the organic whole. A car engine consists of hundreds of assembled parts. Imagine that you had a free afternoon and chose to take apart your car's engine and lay each part on the grass. You would still have the exact same collection of parts, no fewer, no more. Yet, the parts spread across the lawn would neither resemble nor function like a car engine. This is because the parts, in and of themselves, do not constitute a car engine. It is only when the parts are assembled and organized in a certain manner that they become a car engine.

For Bergson and Driesch the principle behind how the parts of the human body, or of any other organism, function was no different.

Indeed, by the end of the nineteenth century it was becoming apparent that the most basic unit of an organism, the cell, was in fact itself a highly complex entity. It was not clear whether each cell should be considered the primary unit of life or whether cells in combination (as whole organisms) should be considered the primary unit. There was no definitive answer because the cell and the organism constituted a system with its own structure and order.

Two conclusions follow from the work of Bergson and Driesch concerning organic structures. First, the idea that a part can exist outside the context of the whole is meaningless. Each part is defined by its relation to other parts within the overall structure of the organism. Analyzing isolated parts is like trying to start your car by rearranging the engine parts on your lawn. The basic unit of analysis is, therefore, the whole and not the part. Second, each whole is itself a part of a larger structure (or system). A system is a pattern of ordered wholes. The human body, for example, is an ordered whole that combines many subsystems—the skeletal system, the immune system, and so on.

Social Structures

It was initially popular to draw direct analogies between the human body as a complex organic system and society as a complex social system. The human body was made up of integrated subsystems (such as the nervous system or the circulatory system) that kept the human organism in balance and facilitated development. Likewise, society was composed of integrated subsystems (such as the kinship system or the economic system) that kept social relations in balance and facilitated development. There was a basic dilemma, however, for those who sought to extend this analogy too far. A cell in the body lacks conscious awareness, while societies are made up of individuals with human subjectivity and free will. A systems-level approach was inconsistent with individual-level autonomy.

For this reason, structuralism raises a fundamental conflict between structural determinism and individual autonomy. To develop this point, it is helpful to imagine a continuum. At one extreme lies structural determinism. All of a person's actions are determined by social context. The individual has no free will to act independently of his or her life's circumstances. At the other extreme lies individual autonomy. All of a person's actions are the result of complete free will. There are no structural constraints on an individual's actions whatsoever. One is free to act how he or she pleases regardless of his or her life's circumstances. Obviously, neither position at the extreme ends of the continuum is entirely plausible. Reconciling the rift between these two extremes is central to the interpretation of social structures as systems.

A central figure early in this debate was Emile Durkheim (1858–1917). Durkheim—whose ideas were strongly influenced by his French compatriot Comte—explored this tension between structural determinism and individual autonomy most fully in *Rules of Sociological Method* (1895) and *Division of Labor in Society* (1893). The issue is generally framed as a conflict between two views of the study of society. On the one hand, there are those who emphasize structural factors and who analyze the qualities and characteristics of the social structures. The nature of individuals in society is explained by the nature of the social structures. On the other hand, there are those who emphasize human subjectivity and who analyze the qualities and characteristics of the individuals who inhabit social structures. The nature of social structures is explained by the nature of individuals in society. The principal difference between the two approaches is one of emphasis. Durkheim was a member of the former camp.

He began by shifting his focus from the individual as the primary unit of analysis to the group. Groups have characteristics that individuals in society do not have, Durkheim suggests. In fact, the group—and not the individual—is the most basic unit of analysis in society. Social facts, therefore, refer to characteristics of groups that do not pertain to individuals. Society is not merely a random assembly of individuals thrown together. Social structures reveal logical patterns and organizational forms. For this reason, various forms of collective social structures (e.g., a mob, the national economy, the Spanish Inquisition) can serve as subjects of study.

For those who emphasize social structures over individuals, structural analysis is essential. Consider two seemingly individual-level decisions: choosing one's clothing fashion and selecting a spouse. In U.S. society, it is the norm that the ultimate decision of how to dress and whom to marry is largely left to the individual. But what role do the pressures of family and friends' expectations play? Structuralists would argue that it certainly seems like a remarkable coincidence that all free-thinking individuals just happen to dress very much like others in their close circle of friends.

These same free-thinking individuals go on to freely choose spouses who, on average, fall within a remarkably narrow range in terms of income, occupation, race, and religion that generally matches their own family's characteristics. So what does it mean to be free to make individual decisions if social pressures are such that they result in a narrow conformity with family and friends' expectations? The only way to explain such a pattern, structuralists argue, is to move the analysis beyond the free will of the individual and onto the level of how social norms are legitimized and enforced through collective social structures.

Cognitive Structures

One of the essential issues that logical positivists—for example, Ernst Mach and Richard Avenarius—grapple with is the process by which a person is able to organize how one experiences the world. (See chapter 2.) This concerns two issues in particular, cognitive processes (how one experiences the world) and intersubjective communication (how one describes what they experience to others). In this regard, the central issue for those investigating cognitive structures is, How does a person organize the conscious thought process and how does he or she use language to express this experience? Linguistics and structural anthropology directly examine cognitive structures. Ferdinand de Saussure (structural linguistics), Claude Lévi-Strauss (1908–1990) (structural anthropology), and Jean Piaget (1896–1980) (structural psychology) are all important figures emphasizing the role of cognitive structures in analysis. Their conceptualizations and theoretical frameworks have guided the development of this area.

There is a critical difference between social structures and cognitive structures that should become clear. Social structuralists analyze group-level structures that shape how social phenomena are interpreted. Cognitive structuralists analyze individual-level structures that shape how social phenomena are interpreted. Both share a common analytical framework that emphasizes how structures shape and define social phenomena. However, the subject matter appropriate to each is distinct, given their respective levels of analysis. Social structuralists examine common sets of rules and principles governing the organization of society. Cognitive structuralists examine common sets of rules and principles governing the organization of individual cognition (how a person understands the social world or human language).

There is a deceptive element to this distinction. Because social structuralists examine society as a whole while cognitive structuralists examine individual cognition, there is a tendency to frame the distinction as one between structural determinists (social structuralists) and individualists (cognitive structuralists). This is erroneous. Cognitive structuralists share the underlying assumptions of their social structure colleagues with regard to the primacy of structure over individual autonomy. Cognitive structuralists merely emphasize such structures at the level of the individual. However, this does not mean that the individual is able to exercise any degree of freedom with respect to the way linguistic structures shape their use of language. Cognitive structures provide a framework for understanding the limited options for individual thought and communication, just as social structuralists provide a framework for understanding the limited options for social groups.

WHAT ARE THE BASIC ELEMENTS OF STRUCTURALISM?

The fundamental premise of structuralism is that the significance of all social phenomena is ultimately determined by their context—their position or role within a complex system. From this basic insight sprang many forms of analysis. It is helpful to limit the broader field of structuralism by organizing the discussion around three specific forms of analysis that have been highly influential within structuralism. Through an examination of the specific features of functionalism, linguistics, and structural anthropology it is possible to delineate the basic features of structuralism in general.

Functionalism

Functionalism concerns the analysis of social structures. A basic premise of functionalism is that societies represent large-scale, complex social systems composed of differentiated and interdependent social structures and practices. Differentiation—the topic of Durkheim's *Division of Labor in Society*—is the degree of specialization among the members of society. Complex societies have highly specialized social structures, such as multitiered labor markets. Interdependence is the degree to which social processes are linked and integrated across society. A national transportation system is an example of a social structure that contributes to interdependence. Complex societies have highly integrated social structures. Thus, as societies develop, they become more specialized and more integrated. One of the differences between U.S. society today and U.S. society two hundred years ago is its highly developed national market economy that coordinates the activity of millions of people across the country.

A second important premise of functionalism is the emphasis on aggregates and wholes. An aggregate refers to a complex system in which the parts are cumulative and divisible. A whole refers to a complex system in which the parts are integrated and indivisible. The parts of a whole are integrated in the sense that, in tandem, the role of each is to maintain the system. The parts of a whole are indivisible in the sense that each relies upon the other. The purpose of each part is, first and foremost, to contribute to the specialization and integration of the larger system. The parts have no significance separate from this role. The goal of functionalism, therefore, is to determine how parts (social structures and social practices) fit the needs of the larger system (society) with respect to differentiation and interdependence.

The Polish anthropologist Bronislaw Malinowski (1884–1942) was the first to systematically employ a functionalist approach in the analysis of cultural systems. This approach was developed, in part, in *The Scientific Theory of Culture* (1922). Malinowski attempts to explain specific cultural practices by identifying the role they play within an integrated cultural system. There are no randomly occurring cultural practices. Each plays an explicit, functional role in promoting order and stability. Malinowski argues that, with sufficient study, one can specify how each cultural practice serves the functional needs of the individuals in that society. Importantly, the stabilizing role of each cultural practice operates at the level of the individual, meeting a person's biological and psychological needs.

Following Malinowki's pioneering studies, several major works further shaped the development of functionalism, which proved especially influential in the U.S. social sciences. These included A. R. Radcliffe-Brown (1881–1955), *Structure and Function in Primitive Society* (1952); Robert Merton (1910–2003), *Social Theory and Social Structure* (1949); Talcott Parsons (1902–1979), *The Social System* (1951); and Kingsley Davis (1908–1997), *Human Society* (1949).

The British anthropologist A. R. Radcliffe-Brown began with Malinowski's basic insights. However, he shifted his analysis from the level of an individual's biological and psychological needs. Instead, he argues that the role of a cultural practice is to promote social stability and the perpetuation of societies as a whole. Cultural practices are analyzed in terms of the contributions they make to the social order rather than the contributions they make to individual well-being.

Consider the example of childbirth. Many societies rely upon midwifery birthing practices that go back many centuries. Malinowski would argue that the role of such practices is to provide comfort and security to a woman through the emotionally and physically demanding process of childbirth. Radcliffe-Brown would argue that the role of such practices goes well beyond an individual woman in childbirth. They help to stabilize social relationships by legitimizing an essential social role for women (as midwives) and to perpetuate the social order by safeguarding an essential social function (childbirth and reproduction).

Radcliffe-Brown made a second, related shift. Malinowski focused on specific cultural items. Radcliffe-Brown pays less attention to individual cultural items and instead concentrates on the organizational pattern of cultural items within a complex social system. He argues that the proper unit of analysis is the social system as a whole. Each social system is made up of a set of interconnected patterns of recurrent relationships. It is at the level of these patterns and relationships that social stability and maintenance are assured. Therefore, it is the actual patterns of recurrent relationships that are functional, not the individual cultural items. This approach, referred to as structural-functionalism, became the dominant approach for social analysis in U.S. sociology through the mid-1960s.

A brief example related to death and bereavement will illustrate the distinction between Malinowski's approach and that of structural-functionalism. All societies have specific cultural items and practices related to death and bereavement. The specific cultural items and practices differ across societies (e.g., style of clothing, length of the grieving period, treatment of the corpse). However, in each case such practices fit within a broader pattern of integrating death and dying into the general social order, promoting stability (common behavioral norms and practices) and continuity (respectful treatment of ancestors). Malinowski emphasizes individual stability and so he analyzes how an individual's participation in ritual practices (cultural items) related to death and dying promotes personal adjustment to a traumatic event. Radcliffe-Brown emphasizes societal stability and so he analyzes how intergenerational, collective practices (patterns of recurrent relationships) related to death and dying promote societal continuity.

The U.S. sociologist Robert Merton expanded upon the work of both Malinowski and Radcliffe-Brown. Merton's contributions to functionalism are many. There are four areas of particular influence. (1) Merton argues that the very concept of function, with respect to social practices, has to be more precisely defined. In line with Radcliffe-Brown, he limits the concept of function to the specific, observable consequences of a social practice. The individual subjective aims associated with social practices are irrelevant. In this way, Merton distinguishes between the actual social role of a social practice and its intended purpose. For example, the actual social role of a grocery store is to facilitate the distribution of food. The intended purpose of someone shopping at a grocery store is to satisfy an individual's momentary needs.

(2) To further sharpen this distinction between the actual role and the intended purpose of social practices, Merton introduces the concepts of manifest and latent functions. Manifest functions are the intended consequences of social practices. Latent functions are the unintended consequences of social practices. This is meant to clarify the distinction between the function and the purpose of a social practice. The function of a social practice is to maintain societal stability. The purpose of a social practice is to satisfy individual needs. Thus, the *function* of marriage (social stability and reproduction) is distinct from the *purpose* of two persons getting married (personal fulfillment). For this reason, Merton emphasizes the latent function of social practices.

(3) Merton notes that the same social practice does not necessarily provide the same level of functional unity in different societies. All societies harbor varying degrees of differentiation and
interdependence. Two societies might have an identical social practice related to kinship structure. However, if one society's social
structures possess greater differentiation and interdependence, then,
it is argued, that social practice will create greater unity across this
society as a whole than it will in the other. This principle also holds
true for different levels within the same society. As a result, some
social practices can be functional at one level and dysfunctional at
another. Sharing money and resources without formal rules and
restrictions is a functional social practice at the level of the family.
However, sharing money and resources in a similar fashion at the
level of a neighborhood may prove to be dysfunctional. This is
due, in part, to different degrees of differentiation and interdependence in a family unit than in a neighborhood.

(4) Lastly, Merton argues that within functionalism there is a
critical distinction between understanding a social practice and
explaining a social practice. Comprehending and describing the
function of a social practice is not the same as accounting for it on
the basis of a general social law. Social practices are not explained
by describing their societal function in the same manner that events
are explained by general social laws. Functionalism provides a form
of explanation that accounts for a social practice based on its role
within a complex system. This does not lend itself to forms of
explanation based on deductive or inductive logic. The meaning of
a specific social practice is determined by the role it plays in the
perpetuation of a given social system. The same social practice
could play an entirely different role in another society. The consequences of social practices—rather than their causes—are of interest within functionalism.

Linguistics

Linguistics concerns the analysis of cognitive structures. In particular, linguistics analyzes the use of language and the nature of
thought processes. Linguistics has had a significant impact on methodological issues in sociology. Both key concepts as well as a good
deal of the language (or terminology) of linguistics have been

adopted by sociologists working in the structural tradition. The story of twentieth-century linguistics generally begins with the Swiss linguist Ferdinand de Saussure and his break from the traditional linguistics of the late nineteenth century. Saussure set out his new approach in a lecture series from 1907 to 1911. This was later published as *Course in General Linguistics* (1915).

Prior to Saussure, the field of linguistics approached the study of language in a manner similar to evolutionary biology. The roots of modern languages were traced historically and languages were understood to develop over time and to influence other languages. The study of language as a developmental form is referred to as diachronic. Saussure's approach to linguistics treated language as a complex system of communication. He sought to understand the nature of language, not as a historical heirloom, but as a system of interpersonal communication. The study of language as a complex communication system is referred to as synchronic. In considering the synchronic approach, Saussure's innovations can be organized around three themes.

(1) Saussure argues that language must be thought of as a systematic organization of symbolic devices (referred to as signs). In spoken language, signs are noises that communicate concepts. They communicate concepts because they are part of a language system that relates certain noises to certain concepts. The noise is the signifier—the sound heard when the word "bird" is spoken. The concept is the signified—the actual animal we know as a bird. Saussure argues that language is a system of signs in which we use signifiers to communicate thoughts about the signified. What noise is linked to what concept is completely arbitrary. The same concept (bird) can have hundreds of different noises associated with it across different languages. However, the underlying structural principle—the use of signifiers and signified—is universal across all languages.

(2) Saussure further argues that it is the underlying structure of language (its internal system of relations) that gives words their meaning. Words are not meaningful in isolation. They only have meaning in relation to other words within the same language system. To "learn" the meaning of a word is to understand how different sounds signify different concepts. This requires knowing the place of a word (or its sound) within the larger system of

language. Within any language system there is some degree of variation. In the United States, the southern dialect and the New England dialect both operate within the same language system and use similar words to refer to similar concepts. However, there are significant differences in pronunciation, indicating that the sound associated with a concept operates within a certain range. Saussure illustrated this point with the example of a chess game. The actual shape and appearance of each chess piece are unimportant. The pieces merely need to be distinguishable in some way. In this manner, each piece is defined, not by any unchanging, universal appearance, but by its relation to other pieces.

(3) Lastly, Saussure argues that there is a difference between language as a complex system and language as an everyday form. *La langue* refers to language as a complex system. From this perspective, language is a social product through which a community's conceptual understanding of the world is interpreted and explained. *Parole* refers to people's actual speech. From this perspective, language is an individual's self-expression that emerges through the use of *la langue* in the form of everyday conversation. While actual speech (*parole*) varies with individuals, language as a system (*la langue*) reveals certain underlying social forms. For this reason, Saussure emphasizes *la langue*.

Franz Boas (1858–1942), in *Handbook of American Indian Languages* (1911), and the Czech Vilem Mathesius (1882–1945) developed versions of Saussure's diachronic approach independently of his work. Mathesius's work in linguistics, emphasizing a synchronic, ahistorical approach, resulted in the establishment of the highly influential Prague school of linguistics in 1926. A central tenet of the Prague school is that the proper analysis of language begins with an understanding of the function of various structural components within a language system. This is referred to as the functional sentence perspective.

The functional sentence perspective attributes functional explanations to different patterns within language. The manner by which information is communicated within a conversation provides an example. Many spoken sentences give information. However, this information is not random. A speaker shares what he or she wants the listener to know based on (a) what the listener already knows and (b) the context of an ongoing conversation. For such a conversation to have any continuity or coherence it must have two parts. (1) The theme is that aspect of a sentence that the listener already knows. (2) The rheme is that aspect of a sentence that is a new fact for the listener within the context of the ongoing conversation.

Roman Jakobson (1896–1982) was a member of the Prague school who moved to the United States in 1941. He further argues that there is an orderly, universal system of sounds that underlies language systems. Whereas others had argued that sounds vary widely between languages, Jakobson maintains that, in fact, there are very few differences between sounds that differentiate words. This limited range of sounds is determined by innate features of the human mind. The notion that innate features of the human mind shape the structure of language systems was extended by Noam Chomsky, a student of Jakobson, to the study of grammar.

Chomsky argues that both the differences between the sounds associated with words in different language systems as well as the differences between the grammar patterns that differentiate language systems from one another are quite small. The similarity of grammar patterns across language systems is evidence of certain innate features of the human mind. To make this point, Chomsky examines how children learn language. Children learn a great deal about the world by observation and by repeating what others say and do. However, children cannot simply learn grammar rules by repeating what they have heard because they are also able to develop sentences that they have never heard. Thus, children possess the innate ability to infer grammar rules. Moreover, children can learn the grammar rules of any language system they happen to grow up in. All language systems must, therefore, share a single, underlying structure that children are born with an innate ability to acquire.

The work of Jakobson and Chomsky represents a significant shift from the earlier linguistic tradition of Saussure. Whereas Saussure and others had focused on differences between language systems as indicators of differences between different societies' structures and organizational practices, Jakobson and Chomsky turn their attention to the origins of organizational patterns of language with an emphasis on the innate mental qualities of individuals. This is a kind of reversal of the functionalist history. Functionalism began with a focus on the individual (Malinowski's approach) and evolved into the study of social structures (Radcliffe-Brown's approach). Linguistics began as the study of language as a complex communication system reflecting societal and cultural differences (Saussure's approach) and evolved into the study of language as a universal set of sounds and grammatical rules attuned to an individual's mental faculties (Jakobson's approach).

Structural Anthropology

Structural anthropology is the study of cultural practices as structured systems. Structural anthropology makes use of the basic insights of Saussure's structural linguistics to study underlying organizational patterns beneath the surface of cultural practices (such as child rearing or religion). The Russian Nicolay Trubetzkoy (1890–1938) was one of the first to develop a framework for applying Saussure's linguistics to the social sciences. This approach was outlined in his posthumously published work, *Principles of Phonology* (1939). Trubetzkoy asserts that a central concern of the social sciences is the social use of material objects. In this respect, it is important to distinguish between an object itself and the object's role within a specific social system. This distinction is similar to that in functionalism between Malinowski's focus on cultural items and Radcliffe-Brown's focus on organizing patterns.

Trubetzkoy argues that, within structuralism, there is a basic distinction between the physical world and the social world. This distinction is evident when analyzing a specific event. With respect to the physical world, a researcher can locate an event according to a specific time and place. (A man robbed the bank on the corner at 4:00 p.m.) With respect to the social world, a social researcher interprets and attributes meaning to an event. (Certain social conditions leave some people so desperate for money that they are willing to rob people to get it.) The social sciences are interested not just in the physical description of the event itself but also in the interpretation of the event and the function that the event plays within a specific social context. Like an isolated word plucked from a language system, an individual event is meaningless outside the context of an underlying social system that gives it meaning.

From this perspective, the pursuit of causal historical explanations—based on the deductive-nomological model discussed in chapter 2—is misplaced. Identifying specific social structures (as complex systems) that bestow meaning on an event provides the only sound basis for interpreting a specific event. Consider the example of civil unrest after a police officer kills an unarmed African American man in a poor African American neighborhood. The unrest can be understood, in part, as an immediate reaction to an officer's behavior. However, the broader structure of race relations and police repression in a particular community may provide a fuller explanation of civil unrest. The social structure (a racially polarized community) is the explanation for civil unrest in this case, and it is very likely that the exact same event in a wealthy, white neighborhood would not have the same results. This is because the event (an officer killing an innocent person) would not have the same racially charged meaning for the white community. Again, the event only has meaning in context.

Structural anthropology has arguably been the most influential form of structural analysis to build on Trubetzkoy's insights. Claude Lévi-Strauss, whose *Structural Anthropology* (1958) provided its impetus, remains the central figure in structural anthropology. In his attempt to directly apply the concepts and terminology of structural linguistics to the study of cultural forms, Lévi-Strauss drew inspiration from Saussure and Trubetzkoy as well as from Jakobson. In these efforts, Lévi-Strauss popularized two innovative techniques for the study of cultures and societies.

(1) To begin, Lévi-Strauss accepted Saussure's treatment of language as a system of signs (signifiers and signified) and set out to apply this principle to the cultural practices that comprise a cultural system. All cultural practices contain embedded symbolic meaning, it is argued. The study of signs within cultural systems is referred to as semiology (or semiotics). Lévi-Strauss argues that there are implicit messages attached to all objects and all actions (verbal or nonverbal) that are specific to a cultural system. Wearing black to a funeral, for example, in some cultures indicates mourning. Just as Saussure argues that a specific sound (or word) can only be interpreted in the context of a broader language system, Lévi-Strauss argues that a specific cultural practice (e.g., religious worship) must be interpreted in the context of a broader cultural system.

(2) Lévi-Strauss incorporates Jakobson's and Chomsky's assertion that there are universal human qualities that allow the mind to

function as a structural template that organizes cultural practices. Just as Jakobson and Chomsky argue that the differences between the sounds for words and the grammars of language systems are small, Lévi-Strauss contends that the differences between cultural practices (e.g., myths or kinship systems) across cultural systems are small. Thus, while the specific details of myths may change, the basic underlying symbolic messages are similar across cultural systems.

Accordingly, just as children's minds are innately predisposed to learn any language's grammar, their minds are prewired to interpret the structural patterns that provide a logic for cultural practices. The capacity to read meaning into patterns of cultural practices is an inherent quality of the human mind. For example, consider cultural practices related to dress and grooming. All societies adopt distinct dress and grooming customs, with styles differing widely across societies. Certain types of differences exist across all societies, however, regarding dress and grooming patterns for females versus males and for children versus elders. When children are confronted with an unfamiliar article of clothing, they are generally able to say whether it is worn by a female or male or whether it belongs to a child or to an elder. It is argued that children are predisposed to develop an understanding of these differences just as they are predisposed to acquire grammar.

This peculiar human faculty exists prior to interacting with a given cultural system and does not derive from it. Because these organizational patterns in the mind precede exposure to the cultural system, they cannot originate in a need to maintain societal stability, as argued by functionalism. By implication, over the course of history only superficial changes can occur across cultures. The underlying structural forms and patterns of cultural practices remain the same for all people, for all time. Historical social change does not alter the mind's innate disposition to interpret and organize distinct cultural practices according to universal structural patterns.

WHAT ARE THE IMPLICATIONS OF STRUCTURALISM?

As is evident, there are many strands and tendencies to contend with when presenting an overview of structuralism as a distinct and coherent form of social analysis. Nonetheless, there are certain core premises that are common across the variations of structural analysis. In particular, there are four premises of structuralism, each of which is further linked to a set of specific implications for social analysis.

(1) The first premise of structuralism concerns the distinction between parts and wholes. From a methodological perspective, a great many consequences follow from the fact that the social world is analyzed via a lens that prioritizes the whole over the parts. Individual social phenomena are of little direct interest. Instead, the importance of any specific social phenomenon is the nature of its relationship to other phenomena and to the social system as a whole. This distinction between parts and wholes shapes how questions about society are investigated and resolved. More importantly, it shapes how such questions are asked. Four implications follow from this premise.

First, a social phenomenon's specific characteristics are less important than its relation to other phenomena and its role in the social system. Little is gained by investing one's time analyzing the minute details of any given social phenomenon if the explanation for it is to be found at the level of the structural context that defines it. For example, there is no reason to bother with the specific events and personalities linked to a lynching in the Jim Crow South when trying to explain why it occurred. The reasons for such a lynching are tied to a social structure premised upon white supremacy. Structural analysis requires a detailed description of the whole (Jim Crow society) not the part (an individual lynching). It is noteworthy that social structures themselves (Jim Crow society) are no more autonomous than individuals in society. Their form and nature are determined by the needs of larger social systems (society following slavery and Reconstruction).

Second, there is an inherent difficulty in precisely defining the level at which a particular social phenomenon is operating. There is the ever present danger with structural analysis that the system one is focused on might be subsumed by another system. Continuing with our example, imagine that the lynching occurred in a specific rural county. This represents a structure within which the event took place. The rural county is itself part of a larger structure, a southern state. In turn, the state is part of a national region, the U.S. South, and so on. Structural analysis must move between various levels of structures (a complex labyrinth of systems and subsystems) to explain specific social phenomena. There is always a certain degree of arbitrariness in determining which level most fully accounts for a given phenomenon.

Third, a distinction emerges between the unit of analysis (the system) and the unit of observation (the part). This is inevitable and follows from the fact that systems cannot be directly observed. Only their parts are visible. A lynching is an isolated event. A pattern of racial discrimination and repression (including lynching) transforms an individual act into evidence of a larger social pattern. The pattern itself cannot be observed. It must be inferred from observations of individual acts (such as a lynching). This is why there is so little interest in the details of an individual lynching. Such a lynching is expected. It is easily anticipated. This follows from the basic distinction between the unit of analysis (the racist social system) and the unit of observation (an individual lynching).

Fourth, a distinction arises between systems as abstract concepts and parts as concrete, observable things. This follows from the previous point regarding units of analysis and units of observation. Structural analysis will, of necessity, take the form of an abstract conceptual explanation. The system at the center of the analysis has no concrete, observable form. As a result, a certain vagueness and distance are inevitable with structural analysis. The horrific details of a lynching are far more moving than a detached description of the broad social structures that create the conditions for it. For this reason, an abstract structural analysis can often leave one uncertain regarding its application and relevance in the real world.

(2) The second premise of structuralism revolves around the issue of structural determinism. Structural determinism refers to the tendency to attribute the actions of individuals to the rules and governing logic of a complex social system rather than to a person's own subjective decision making. As discussed in the earlier example of choosing one's personal fashion or a marital partner, there is always a balance to be drawn between one's degree of personal free will and the societal pressures that frame individual decisions. Erring on the side of structural determinism discounts the role of individuals in shaping society. Erring on the side of individual autonomy discounts the role of social structures in shaping society. Two implications follow from structural determinism.

First, there is a tendency to account for a specific social phenomenon through an appeal to the nature—and needs—of a complex social system rather than the actions of an autonomous individual. The vast majority of people in the United States who choose to become nurses happen to be women. We know that there are no armed gangs roaming the back roads in pickup trucks and forcibly rounding up women to be nursing candidates. The decision to become a nurse remains an individual choice. A structural argument would point to the gender division of labor in the medical field or popular customs and practices that link nurses (as nurturers) to the traditional societal role of women (as nurturers). There is no effort to analyze how each woman who opts to be a nurse grapples with these issues in her own conscience. Structural considerations (e.g., the gender division of labor, the role of popular customs) take precedence over any concern for individual subjectivity as an explanation for why most nurses are women in U.S. society.

Second, it logically follows that to account for a specific social phenomenon there is little or no need to consider the motives, interests, or ideas of individuals. Imagine that it is possible to conduct a survey in which it is discovered that those who chose to become nurses exhibited a significantly greater desire to provide nurturing care than the general public. In short, the survey demonstrates that there is a strong link between a person's choosing to become a nurse and a person's individual-level desire to provide nurturing care. Again, the structuralist remains ready to swoop down and snatch individual subjectivity from our grasp. It is argued, quite simply, that it is fully expected that there will be a strong correlation between the desire to nurture and the desire to become a nurse. That is the nature of the nursing profession in U.S. society. However, the fact that women disproportionately desire to nurture is itself a result of social structures shaping gender roles in society.

(3) The third premise of structuralism celebrates the triumph of reason over empiricism. Within structuralism, empirical evidence does not guide the analysis. Rather, there is a tendency for the analysis to shape the interpretation of empirical evidence. This is directly related to the emphasis on wholes over parts. Specific social phenomena are explained by their role within social struc-

tures. As a consequence, reason (a structural argument) is difficult to defeat through a response based on empirical evidence at the level of social phenomena. Rather, to overturn a structural argument requires developing a competing structural argument that better accounts for social phenomena within the logic of its structure. Two implications follow from this premise.

First, there is the danger of falling into tautological error. Tautological error occurs when the premises of one's argument assume what one wishes to prove. One begins by positing a structural argument and proceeds to characterize social phenomena in a manner that is consistent with one's argument. This results in self-fulfilling prophecies. Consider the impact of European colonial rule in Africa throughout the nineteenth and twentieth centuries. It has been argued that the pattern of European domination over African peoples' lives, resources, and social institutions contributed to the abysmal state of late-twentieth-century African development. All social phenomena deemed injurious to African development (such as endemic interethnic conflict due to arbitrary national borders) are summarily attributed to the impact of colonial rule. Clearly, colonial rule contributed greatly to the current state of African development. However, basing one's analysis of all contemporary conditions in Africa on this alone eliminates the need for any actual analysis beyond characterizing each instance to fit a predetermined conclusion.

Second, it is exceedingly difficult to produce counterfactual examples that refute a conclusion based on structural analysis. This also follows from the tautological nature of structural arguments. One discovers that there is actually no such thing as a counterexample. There are only counterarguments that might better account for a certain example. Not all postcolonial African societies fared equally poorly. Some did better than others. For instance, there are significant differences between postcolonial African societies that were controlled by Portugal and those controlled by the British. A person searching for a counterexample might fasten onto these differences to suggest that, because colonial rule was present in both cases, something else must account for the differences.

The structuralist would respond that any differences between the social institutions in Angola (a former Portuguese colony) and those in Nigeria (a former British colony) are not evidence that colonial rule does not account for underdevelopment. Rather, it is evidence that there were differences between forms of colonial rule (as social systems) based on which European power had established the colony. In this case, one structural argument (an indictment of colonial rule in general) is superseded by a second structural argument. The second structural argument continues to attribute twentieth-century African underdevelopment to European colonial rule. However, it has absorbed an apparent counterexample by recognizing that the specific form of colonial rule—and thus its specific impact on African societies—varied depending upon which European power was in charge.

(4) The fourth premise of structuralism points to a general reliance on ahistorical and universal structures. This follows from the fact that the role of structures is to serve the developmental needs of complex systems. This neutralizes historical change and mutes social conflict. There is no historical change because a structure premised on promoting self-perpetuation, by definition, develops no dynamic for change. The ruling ethos is self-preservation. Social conflict is muted because systems are, by definition, made up only of parts that are amenable to its ends. Conflictual parts would not serve any role in the system and would not develop. As a consequence, in the case of social systems, those structures that do emerge are considered to be ahistorical. Historical events do not shape social systems. Social systems shape historical events. Similarly, in the case of cognitive systems, the structures are considered to be universal. Linguistic analysis attempts to identify underlying structural patterns that are universal across language systems. Two implications follow from this premise.

First, when analyzing social structures, there is a tendency to emphasize continuity and consistency rather than discontinuity and inconsistency. Beginning in the 1960s, there was a concerted effort to account for the process of modernization in countries outside the advanced industrial world. It was widely held that each society had to go through specific stages to fully develop its economic, political, and social institutions. A society could be monitored as it progressed through these stages. The development of these countries was considered to be consistent with the previous developmental pattern of advanced industrial countries. The entire process represented a clear continuity between the earlier modernization experience and the contemporary one. Development that was inconsistent with the established stages of modernization was explained away as an error or misunderstanding on the part of the developing society.

Second, when analyzing social structures, there is a tendency to emphasize common characteristics and shared traits rather than differences or unique circumstances. After all, if structures and systems are ahistorical and have universal features, then differences and unique circumstances are irrelevant. In the case of the stages of modernization, many social structures must exist to secure a developing country's path to prosperity. All of these structures have been taken directly from advanced industrial societies, including a vibrant market economy, an open political system, an active press, a strong banking and financial sector, and a flourishing civil society. In this regard, the goal of modernization is to cast underdeveloped countries in the precise image of advanced industrial countries. The goal is to look past differences (such as a country's location in the world economy) and to ignore unique circumstances (such as centuries of colonial rule). As a result, a universal prescription is offered to all developing countries based on an ahistorical, structural analysis of modernization.

FURTHER READING

Bottomore, Tom, and Robert Nisbett. "Structuralism." Pp. 557–99 in *A History of Sociological Analysis.* Edited by Tom Bottomore and Robert Nisbett. New York: Basic Books, 1978.

Giddens, Anthony. "Structuralism, Poststructuralism, and the Production of Culture." Pp. 73–109 in *Social Theory and Modern Society.* Stanford: Stanford University Press, 1987.

Moore, Wilbert. "Functionalism." Pp. 321–362 in *A History of Sociological Analysis.* Edited by Tom Bottomore and Robert Nisbett. New York: Basic Books, 1978.

Polkinghorne, Donald. "Systems and Structures." Pp. 135–69 in *Methodology for the Human Sciences.* Albany: SUNY Press, 1983.

Runciman, Walter. "What Is Structuralism?" Pp. 189–283 in *The Philosophy of Social Explanation.* Edited by Alan Ryan. London: Oxford University Press, 1973.

5

Hermeneutics

Hermeneutics provides a way of trying to make sense of the world around us. To follow the arguments within hermeneutics it is necessary, above all, to understand the nature of the problem its proponents set out to address. The entire enterprise revolves around the claim that there are fundamental differences between the types of phenomena that are studied by the physical sciences (inanimate, physical objects) and the types of phenomena studied by the social sciences (human beings). The principal distinction between inanimate objects and human beings is human subjectivity. Given that the concept of human subjectivity plays a pivotal role throughout this chapter, a precise understanding of its use is essential. "Subjectivity" is a shorthand reference for various forms of human expression. These can include emotions, ideas, desires, etc. Subjectivity refers to whatever meaning people attach to their words, thoughts, or actions.

It follows from this that how phenomena are explained by the physical sciences differs considerably from how phenomena are explained in the social sciences. Consider the many ways to destroy a town. A volcano could erupt and bury the town. A riot might get out of control and ravage the town. In the case of a volcano, a researcher could identify a causal chain of geological events leading to the eruption. In the case of a riot, a researcher could also identify a causal chain of events leading to the riot. However, in the case of the riot, the causal chain will necessarily incorporate a number of subjective judgments on the part of the researcher regarding the rioters' actions. Why were the rioters upset? Why did they react in this manner? Why didn't they stop? The geologist has no similar concern for the subjectivity of the volcano. This need to account for the subjectivity of human beings is the principal difference between the physical and social sciences.

Human subjectivity reflects a person's essential purpose and understanding of who he or she is. For this reason, it is necessary to consider how proponents of hermeneutics define the nature of human beings. Humans are intentional beings who create meaningful social phenomena. Four consequences follow from this statement. First, human beings are intentional, creative beings. This implies that a human being is someone who consciously and purposely creates things, whether small items (like a hammer or a sandwich) or large-scale items (like a hospital or an economic system). The essential point is that, by their nature, humans are beings who purposely create things.

Second, the things that people create have meaning, they are meaningful social phenomena. This implies that all those things that people create—the hammers, the sandwiches, the hospitals, the economic systems—are expressions of their subjectivity. A painting, for instance, is the expression of an artist's subjectivity (thoughts, feelings, ideas). For this reason, we can study any social phenomenon (as an outward expression) to understand the thoughts and feelings (the subjectivity) of whoever created it.

Third, human subjectivity operates at both the level of the individual and the level of society. That is, human beings create things both as individuals (hammers and sandwiches) and as members of societies (hospitals and economic systems). When someone writes a book, we can consider the book to be an expression of that person's subjectivity. The meaning and significance of that book is tied to the author as its creator. If a society constructs a series of giant pyramids, then those pyramids are an expression of that society's subjectivity. The meaning and significance of those pyramids is tied to the specific society that created them.

This point can be taken a step further. The proponents of hermeneutics argue that to fully understand the meaning of a book, one must first analyze the historical and cultural circumstances in which the author lived and identify the author's position in society. In this way, the book is seen as an expression of the author's individual subjectivity as well as an expression of the historical and cultural circumstances in which the author lived. In other words, Charles Dickens (1812–1870) the person is as much a product of nineteenth-century England as *A Tale of Two Cities* (1859) is a product of Charles Dickens.

Fourth, the notion of meaningful social phenomena constitutes a very broad category. The term refers to any physical artifact that is a human creation. In addition, meaningful social phenomena can be any form of communication, verbal or nonverbal (a wink, a nod, or a shrug). Literally any human creation falls into this category and can be analyzed for its meaning. The purpose of hermeneutics is to understand how any specific social phenomenon can be thought of as an outward expression of human subjectivity. Hermeneutics, therefore, must provide a researcher with a sound basis for understanding the subjective meaning behind a wide array of contemporary and historical social phenomena. This constitutes a systematic process of interpretation. Researchers are asked to interpret the meaning behind various social phenomena in a manner that will reveal the hidden subjectivity of the original creators of the phenomena.

WHAT ARE THE ORIGINS OF HERMENEUTICS?

Hermeneutics is the product of a great many influences that have been pasted together in a less than systematic fashion over the past couple of centuries. Four historical legacies have played particularly prominent roles. (1) Throughout the Reformation and into the Enlightenment, Europeans were obsessed with a collection of ancient texts that were commonly considered to provide the essential cultural-intellectual foundation of Western civilization. These works included the Bible and various classical works from Greek and Roman antiquity. Fierce debates emerged concerning the true meaning of these works and an entire intellectual enterprise developed that was dedicated solely to their interpretation. The techniques and language from these interpretive efforts eventually formed a basic framework for hermeneutics.

(2) The German contribution to the development of hermeneutics has been especially influential. Many of the modern debates

associated with hermeneutics first emerged in Germany in the nineteenth century. Thus, when outlining the origins of hermeneutics, one cannot ignore the unique role of German thinkers. Beginning with the folkloric and literary works of the German philosopher Johann Gottfried Herder (1744–1803) and the German writer Johann Wolfgang Goethe (1749–1832), through the geopolitical posturing of Otto von Bismarck (1815–1898), the challenge of forging a unified German identity through the reconstitution of common cultural and historical roots galvanized the Germans for nearly two centuries.

(3) In a related matter, hermeneutics has been deeply influenced by the late-nineteenth-century and early-twentieth-century debates concerning the German concept of *verstehen*. This term is generally translated as "understanding." The principal issue in the verstehen debates of interest to a consideration of hermeneutics concerns the conceptual distinction between the role of explanation and the role of understanding (verstehen) within scientific inquiry. It is argued that the physical sciences require methods of analysis that provide explanations, while the social sciences require methods of analysis that provide understanding.

(4) Lastly, hermeneutics has been significantly influenced by developments in the field of phenomenology. Phenomenology is a philosophical movement with origins in the early twentieth century. Its primary concern is how exactly we are able to recognize and navigate the world around us. Phenomenological depictions of how human beings make sense of their experiences has had a profound impact on hermeneutics.

These four factors—the interpretation of classical texts, the German influence, the verstehen debates, and phenomenology—are considered here in the context of the origins of hermeneutics.

The Interpretation of Classical Texts

Early on, the Protestants proved themselves a troublesome lot. Particularly annoying were the imprudent claims of Martin Luther (1483–1546) that Christians could gain a great deal from reading the Bible by themselves outside the direction of the church. The Council of Trent (1545–1563) was held, in part, to formalize the Catholic Church's response to the Protestant Reformation and its attacks on church authority. The council concluded that, in fact, the Bible could only be understood in the context of church tradition and that, therefore, the church alone had the ability to interpret its meaning. Protestants continued to argue that the truths of the Bible could be understood independent of church tradition. However, if this was the case, then it was necessary to devise procedures for interpreting the biblical text outside the context of the church.

Taking on this challenge, Matthias Flacius (1520–1575), a Lutheran reformer, developed a set of rules and guidelines for individuals to interpret the Bible. In *Clavis Scripturae Sacrae* (1567), Flacius laid out his basic argument that no specific section of the Bible could be understood in isolation. Its meaning depended upon its context in the Bible as a whole. Further debates ensued regarding just how unified the Bible actually was. Did all the books of the Bible need to be read in relation to one another or did they stand on their own as separate texts? This fundamental issue of how parts relate to wholes when interpreting a given text remains a central debate within hermeneutics.

The interpretation of classical works from Greek and Roman antiquity presented a second area of concern during the post-Renaissance period. Many European intellectuals considered these works from Greek and Roman classical periods to be a primary source for many Western cultural traditions. How a sixteenth-century reader was to make sense of these texts from antiquity raised a great many issues. Sophisticated techniques of interpretation were called upon to resurrect an original text's meaning in the context of its author's cultural setting. Similar issues arose among legal scholars working with historical documents of jurisprudence. These efforts at interpretation proved to be critical forerunners of hermeneutics.

The German theologian Friedrich Schleiermacher (1768–1834) was one of the first to appeal to this post-Renaissance tradition in an effort to develop modern techniques for interpreting texts. Schleiermacher is generally credited with organizing the various hermeneutic techniques that were in use in the early nineteenth-century into a coherent field of inquiry. He provided a bridge from the earlier era to the present. For Schleiermacher, hermeneutics concerns the problem of historical knowledge and how someone from one period can understand someone from a previous period.

He argues that interpreting an author's work requires submerging oneself in the totality of the author's life circumstances. This empathetic approach involves both a linguistic element, in which one analyzes a text with regard to the author's original language, and a sociohistorical element, in which one analyzes a text with regard to the author's historical life circumstances. In this regard, an interpreter must delve into all the aspects of the author's life that helped shape the expressions and meanings in the author's writing.

The German Influence

Following the publication of *Critique of Pure Reason* (1781), the ideas of the German philosopher Immanuel Kant (1724–1804) assumed a position of supreme dominance in German intellectual circles. All debate turned on consideration of this influential text and its central thesis. In this work, Kant set out to provide the definitive foundation for all scientific knowledge. To do so, he maintained that certain categories of knowledge—those that made scientific inquiry possible—were equally applicable to both the physical and the social sciences. In other words, despite any differences in their immediate subject matter, the physical and social sciences could rely upon a common method of scientific inquiry.

A generation later, the German historian Johann Gustav Droysen (1808–1884) took strong issue with Kant's characterization. In *Outlines of the Principles of History* (1858), Droysen argues that, in fact, there is a fundamental distinction between the physical and social sciences. This distinction follows the same lines as that between the role of *erklären* (explanation) and the role of *verstehen* (understanding) in methods of inquiry. This marked an initial volley in the so-called verstehen debates. Droysen holds that the nature of the physical sciences is such that they attempt to explain physical phenomena by appealing to universal laws. The nature of the social sciences is such that they attempt to provide an understanding of social phenomena through interpretation. In this sense, the two require distinct types of knowledge.

The German social philosophers Wilhelm Windelband (1848–1915) and Heinrich Rickert (1863–1936) expanded on Droysen's call for a methodological distinction between the physical and social sciences. Windelband formalized the distinction by distinguishing between nomothetic and idiographic methods as conceptually incompatible forms of investigation. The nomothetic approach, appropriate for the physical sciences, relies upon causality and explanation. The idiographic approach, appropriate for the social sciences, relies upon the detailed study of unique, individual cases to understand each case's specific meaning and characteristics. In *Culture Science and Natural Science* (1889), Rickert took this a step further and emphasized the study of concrete, individual cases as cultural products. Rickert advocates investigating cultural products and social institutions to better understand human societies as a whole.

Arguably the most influential of those analyzing the differences between the physical and social sciences at end of the nineteenth century was the German social philosopher Wilhelm Dilthey (1833–1911). Dilthey's major work in this regard is *Introduction to the Human Sciences* (1883). Here, Dilthey extends the general argument that a human being is more than a physiobiological creature. Humans are endowed with a subjectivity that is expressed in forms that are not amenable to the rationale governing the physical laws of nature. In addition, individuals do not live in isolation. For this reason, human subjectivity can only be understood in the broader context of a person's social and cultural life—what is referred to as the individual's life-world. Prior to Dilthey, hermeneutic analysis had been largely limited to the interpretation of texts or legal arguments. Dilthey expanded hermeneutic analysis from this initial narrow scope. He broadened the subject matter of hermeneutics to the study of the meaning behind almost any social phenomenon, arguing that all phenomena created by people are, by definition, expressions of human subjectivity. Dilthey's contributions can be organized around two general themes.

(1) Dilthey argues that experience of the social world is organized by unique frames of reference that guide people. He referred to these frames as categories of life. In other words, people do not experience the world as a random, incoherent blur of sensations. Somehow our everyday experiences appear to us as organized and understandable. A central project of the hermeneutics researcher, according to Dilthey, is to uncover these principles of organization. He believes that, by examining the life-world in depth, a researcher can identify patterns that shape how we experience the world and

make sense of things. This requires re-creating the precise social and cultural conditions under which someone created a specific social phenomenon—such as the earlier example of Dickens and *A Tale of Two Cities.*

(2) Dilthey devised his categories of life in direct challenge to Kant. He sought to answer Kant's critique of pure reason with his own critique of historical reason. By this, Dilthey means that the categories of life through which we make sense of the world must be understood historically and cannot be treated as universal perspectives, as Windelband and Rickert insisted. Kant developed categories of understanding to explain how a person's mind is able to construct order in the physical world. This is how one is able to discern that an object has a shape and size. What is an apple and what is an orange is determined by human convention and what we happen to call different things in the world. However, according to Kant, the ability to distinguish between the shape and texture of an apple and those of an orange is an innate human quality and is not learned.

These categories are, therefore, universal (they are the same for all human beings) and they exist prior to a person's experience of the physical world. Indeed, they are what allow us to have our first experience of the physical world. Dilthey argues that human beings use a similar set of categories to experience the social world. These are frames of reference that allow us to make sense of social situations—to recognize when someone is angry with us, frightened, or acting dangerously. Dilthey argues, however, that these categories are not universal and that they do not exist prior to our experience. Rather, they are historical and determined by specific historical settings and cultural traditions. As a consequence, how individuals experience and understand the world is determined by the social and cultural conventions that happen to be used in their society. The meaning they attach to something they create will be similarly affected by these social and cultural conventions.

The Verstehen Debates

Like hermeneutics, the concept of verstehen emerged from nineteenth-century debates concerning the essential differences between the physical and social sciences. The German sociologist Max Weber (1864–1920), among others, argued that the principal purpose of social science is to examine meaningful human action. In this regard, human action has both a visible, physical quality and a hidden, meaningful quality. This is precisely what distinguishes the physical sciences and social sciences. The purpose of the physical sciences is to examine a variety of physical phenomena with no hidden, meaningful qualities (such as the volcano discussed earlier). The physical sciences investigate their subject matter through direct observation. For this, it is sufficient to rely upon one's ordinary understanding. The social sciences also rely upon this type of ordinary understanding to observe and measure human action. However, in addition they must rely upon a form of understanding that allows insight into the hidden meaning behind human action. By convention, this second form of understanding is referred to with the German word *verstehen,* which here can be thought of as interpretive understanding.

Human action, in this sense, is defined as intentional and meaningful human behavior. This distinguishes it from the physical action that is required to carry out a meaningful action. For example, to run down the street is a physical action. However, to flee from an insurance conference as you are chased by eager insurance agents is a meaningful action. Ordinary understanding is sufficient to recognize the physical action of running down the street. Verstehen is necessary to recognize that a person is escaping from an annoying situation. Verstehen, therefore, requires a degree of interpretation that ordinary understanding does not.

This interpretation occurs on two levels. On the one hand, we all use what is called verstehen throughout an ordinary day to interpret people's facial expressions, their tone of voice, body language, etc. This requires minimal reflection and can lead to common cultural misunderstanding. If certain facial expressions are commonly interpreted one way in your home culture and you travel to a culture that interprets the same expressions differently, there can be a good deal of confusion. For example, in U.S. culture a person signals another person to approach by motioning with the palm toward him- or herself. In Japanese culture, the motioning is done with the palm toward the person being beckoned. Verstehen can also be used as a data-gathering tool—a far more complex use of verstehen than the everyday variety.

As a data-gathering tool, verstehen is concerned with devising methods for accurately interpreting the meaning behind specific human actions. This requires a form of systematic reflection on human experience itself. At the center of this method of investigation is the interpretation of meaning that is hidden behind human action. Hermeneutics emerged, in part, as a conscious effort to develop a more refined tool for investigating verstehen. Proponents of hermeneutics helped develop a set of formal rules and procedures to guide the researcher through the process of interpretation. It attempts to guard against a researcher's introduction of subjective judgments while investigating verstehen.

Phenomenology and the Social Sciences

The principal concern of phenomenology is to understand how the human mind organizes experience and makes it accessible to individuals in their everyday lives. Beginning with the German philosopher Edmund Husserl (1859–1938), it has been argued that there are certain essential structures inside a person's consciousness that give form and meaning to the world around us. These essential structures are ever present in everyday life experiences. To reveal these structures requires a systematic method of investigation. This is the purpose of phenomenology. Husserl's major work, the three-volume *Logical Investigations* (1900), introduces the major themes of phenomenology.

Husserl begins with a key distinction between the world of phenomena that make up a person's experience and the essential structures of consciousness through which a person is able to make sense of the world. Importantly, the essential structures are the same for everyone and they exist prior to any exposure to the world of objects. Consciousness of the world and the actual world are, therefore, treated as separate realms. Consciousness does not add anything to the world of objects. It merely frames a person's daily experience in a manner that organizes the flood of experiences into recognizable entities. Husserl sought to develop a method of inquiry to explore the world of pure consciousness where these essential structures reside.

Husserl's phenomenological method of inquiry involves a process called free imaginative variation. In this process, an object is lifted from experience and isolated for detailed study. The goal is (1) to identify those features of the phenomenon that are unique to it and (2) to understand the structures used by consciousness to constitute the phenomenon. Any phenomenon in the world can be reduced to a finite set of essential features that represents its core essence. The first step is to distinguish between a phenomenon's essential and nonessential features. For example, there are many styles and models of cars. It is argued, however, that were one to properly investigate, one could discover a finite set of essential features that describes all cars regardless of style and model differences (e.g., a steering wheel, a driver compartment, an engine). Thus, it is ultimately possible to distinguish a car (no matter its unique style) from a coffin (no matter its unique style).

Once a specific phenomenon has been reduced to its most essential features, it is possible to turn the investigation back to the question of exactly how the essential structures of consciousness organize our experience of this phenomenon. This is referred to as intentional analysis. What allows the essential structures of consciousness to distinguish between our experience of a car and our experience of a coffin? Husserl argues that consciousness has unique properties that allow it to distinguish between a car and a coffin and that these properties exist prior to any experience with a car or a coffin. These structures of consciousness are somehow able to recognize that the two phenomena differ in some essential manner and, on that basis, consciousness is able to organize a person's everyday experiences.

The German sociologist Alfred Schutz (1899–1959) extended Husserl's basic insights to the study of society. In particular, Schutz was concerned with clarifying certain propositions regarding social action. In his major work *The Phenomenology of the Social World* (1932), Schutz examines the nature of social reality as a collection of phenomena that result from a complex interaction of individual social actors. Society is composed of persons (subjective beings) with an individual consciousness whose actions have meaning both to themselves and to others. Society, therefore, constitutes a dynamic world of constantly interacting individuals. Social reality is the product of these interactions and the question is how to investigate the social reality that is driven by this complex combination of individual consciousnesses. Schutz wants to understand how individual, subjective consciousness shapes social action. To do so, he applies Husserl's method of phenomenological investigation to social phenomena in the hope of reducing each social phenomenon to its most essential features.

The work of the German philosopher Martin Heidegger (1889–1976) marks a major turning point in phenomenology. In *Being and Time* (1927), Heidegger argues that Husserl erred in trying to separate the study of essential structures of consciousness from the realm of empirical phenomena. Heidegger maintains that the structures of consciousness do not exist prior to encountering the empirical realm. Consciousness is, in fact, a product of human experience. Heidegger turns his attention to what he calls the being-in-the-world. By this, he means that there are certain aspects of being a human being—such as one's historical life circumstances or knowledge of one's own mortality—that shape consciousness. Accordingly, Husserl's essential structures of consciousness actually originate in a person's lived experience rather than in some realm of pure consciousness. They do not exist prior to experience.

This position is referred to as existential-phenomenology to distinguish it from Husserl's rationalist-phenomenology. It is a view shared—and expanded upon—by the French philosophers Jean-Paul Sartre (1905–1980) and Maurice Merleau-Ponty (1908–1961). Existential-phenomenology argues that the essential structures of consciousness are not based on any a priori rational, logical order. Rather, essential structures of consciousness—the categories that a person uses to organize everyday experiences—are constructed from meaningful human experience. To understand these structures requires reflection and interpretation to uncover a person's lived experiences. Both the rationalist-phenomenology of Husserl and the existential-phenomenology of Heidegger have been highly influential for the development of hermeneutics.

WHAT ARE THE MAIN ELEMENTS OF HERMENEUTICS?

Neatly outlining the main elements of hermeneutics is no simple task. Nonetheless, there are certain recurrent themes and a handful of social philosophers whose debates figure prominently. There is always a certain degree of randomness, however, in organizing these themes and debates. In an effort to cover the breadth of this material, this section is organized into four broad categories: (1) Heidegger, human nature, and the distortions of objective truth, (2) Gadamer and the weight of traditions, (3) Habermas and the influence of social inequality and (4) Dilthey's defenders. Each category introduces key concepts and issues in the context of ongoing debates within hermeneutics.

Heidegger, Human Nature, and the Distortions of Objective Truth

The shadow of Heidegger has been ever present across hermeneutics since the 1930s. It is, therefore, necessary to expand on the previous remarks about Heidegger and to consider the influence of his basic philosophy in greater detail. In *Being and Time* (1927), Heidegger seeks nothing less than complete rupture with a cardinal principle of Western philosophical tradition from the time of René Descartes: the premise that the human mind is a type of mirror that reflects the world around us. Positivist scientific inquiry is based on this notion and seeks to develop techniques of observation that lead to a more accurate reflection. Heidegger rejects the notion of a mirror. Rather, he believes that the human mind is built to creatively interpret—and not to objectively reflect—the world around us.

This basic reformulation was transformative. If the mind, in fact, interprets rather than reflects the world, then there is no basis for believing that certain techniques will provide a more accurate view of the world. Rather, to better understand the world it is necessary to better understand this process of interpretation. For centuries the question had been: How do we know this to be true? The question now became: Why do we interpret the truth to be this?

Dilthey had framed the hermeneutic agenda in line with the dominant Western philosophical traditions. He thought of the mind as a mirror and of hermeneutics as a method to provide a better reflection of the world. Heidegger argues that this is misguided. The field of hermeneutics is actually just a manifestation of human nature. Here it is useful to return to the chapter's original premise: to follow the arguments within hermeneutics it is helpful to keep one's focus on how an author defines the nature of human beings.

Dilthey and the hermeneutic tradition prior to Heidegger define a human being as someone who creates meaningful things. Hermeneutics is a method to understand the meaning behind these things.

Heidegger defines a human being as someone who interprets the world. Heidegger, of course, agrees that human beings create meaningful things. However, this is not the *primary* activity of a human being. Their primary activity is to try to make sense of meaningful things in the world around them. Of course, "trying to make sense of meaningful things in the world" is basically the definition of hermeneutics. Therefore, Heidegger argues that hermeneutics is not some abstract method but simply a description of human nature, an account of what we do every day. There is no more need to teach a person the techniques of hermeneutics than to teach a fish to swim.

There is an important consequence based on the distinction between Dilthey's notion of human nature and Heidegger's notion. In traditional scientific inquiry, true understanding results from distancing oneself from the world one is observing through objective analysis. The more we are able to establish that our results are untainted by observer bias the more accurate is our observation. However, if Heidegger is correct and the human mind can only provide an interpretation of the world, then the opposite is the case. True understanding can only occur when one is fully engaged in the world being observed. Subjective interpretation—and not objective analysis—is the basis for establishing true understanding.

To illustrate this upside-down notion, consider your two friends Xavier and Felix. Xavier loves movies and has seen all the latest ones. Felix is very busy and never goes to movies. One night, the three of you decide to see a movie. Afterward, you sit and discuss it. Xavier's perspective is greatly biased by the many movies he has seen. Felix's perspective is relatively objective and free of bias. Heidegger would argue that it is precisely because Xavier has a highly biased perspective that his subjective interpretation of the movie will represent a truer understanding. Felix's opinion will not be biased by the many films that Xavier has seen. Yet, his views will be less valued precisely because he has little basis for subjective interpretation. For Heidegger truth emerges from constant reference to one's subjective biases, not from ignoring them and pretending they don't exist.

Gadamer and the Weight of Tradition

The analysis of the German philosopher Hans-Georg Gadamer (1900–2002) builds on that of Heidegger. He rejects Dilthey's efforts to obtain a true, unvarnished picture of human subjectivity and accepts Heidegger's notion of human nature. In *Truth and Method* (1960), Gadamer sets out a definitive vision for hermeneutics that breaks with earlier efforts. In concert with Heidegger, Gadamer rejects the notion that truth is revealed through objective techniques that distance the researcher from what he or she is trying to understand. Gadamer does not want to fashion a hermeneutic method to reveal the truth. He wants to use hermeneutics to help clarify the conditions under which understanding occurs. To do so, he emphasizes the influence of past and present traditions on how one understands the world.

There are three notions introduced by Gadamer. (1) The first concerns what Gadamer refers to as the act of mediating past and present "horizons." Consistent with the views of earlier generations, Gadamer believes that the purpose of hermeneutics is to understand the subjective meaning of things that human beings create. Such understanding occurs through interpretation. However, the interpreter harbors his or her own subjective biases. Therefore, when the act of interpretation takes place, there are two subjectivities to account for—that of the creator and that of the interpreter. The subjectivity of the interpreter reflects prejudices and biases, which then influence the interpretation. Gadamer referred to this subjective perspective as the interpreter's horizon. Likewise, the subjective perspective of the person who created the thing being interpreted is that person's horizon. Gadamer thus views hermeneutics as a mediation between a past horizon (the prejudices and biases of the original creator) and a present horizon (the prejudices and biases of the interpreter). Elsewhere, Gadamer refers to mediation as the "fusion" of horizons.

The traditions that shape an interpreter's understanding of the world—for example, the cultural, historical, and social position of the interpreter—are integral and cannot be left out of the hermeneutic process, or neutralized as Dilthey sought. Indeed, the prejudices and biases introduced by these traditions provide the bases for hermeneutic investigation—just as Xavier's extensive movie background gave him greater insights than Felix. Schleiermacher and Dilthey sought to reconstruct the life-world of past creators and to thereby understand their subjectivity. Gadamer seeks to mediate between the subjectivity of past creators and the subjectivity of present interpreters. Put simply, prejudice is good. It is a necessary precondition for any understanding. Thus, ironically, prejudices are not barriers to understanding. They are the bases for making judgments. Having prejudices simply reflects the fact that one is a subjective human being influenced by the historical and cultural traditions that make up one's life-world.

Consider the women's suffrage movement in the United States. Imagine that you want to understand why people opposed women voting in the early twentieth century. For Gadamer, it is not sufficient to reconstruct the life-world of such people to understand their subjectivity. Of equal importance is the life-world of the interpreter. Interpretations of opposition to women's suffrage written in the 1930s, the 1950s, and the 1990s, Gadamer argues, will each present different insights and will each be influenced by different sets of traditions. Perhaps, given their generational proximity, interpreters in the 1930s had a more sympathetic understanding of the issues motivating opposition to women's suffrage than interpreters in the 1990s. But why should such interpretations in the 1990s differ from those in the 1930s? There was nothing necessarily new about the facts in the suffrage debate. The differences, for Gadamer, reflect a mediation of the interpreters' own subjectivities (their horizons). This process of mediation is ongoing and never complete. It is marked by both continuity (due to the deep influence of past tradition) and change (due to evolving cultural and historical conditions).

(2) The second notion introduced by Gadamer concerns his insistence on a plurality of meanings. This follows from the fact that interpreters' own subjectivity can influence their understanding of the past. A phenomenon from the past is not some passive, inert entity. It is open to many interpretations and our understanding of it will shift over the years. Interpretations of past phenomena will simultaneously expose both past meanings and present prejudices and biases. Interpretation is always temporary. It opens a kind of dialogue with the past that will be continued by later interpreters. Rather than a single, unassailable truth, a plurality of meanings emerges from this dialogue.

Again, Dilthey's goal was to recapture the original meaning of a past individual's subjectivity. The fact that varying interpreters (from different time periods or cultural backgrounds) arrive at varying interpretations of the same event is evidence that it has no single, fixed meaning. No interpretation is necessarily more accurate. Each simply reflects the subjectivity of a different interpreter. As an event or text goes through more and more interpretations, its meaning—and our understanding—evolves further. Dilthey argues that a well-crafted interpretation brings us closer to truth. Gadamer counters that this merely brings us closer to an understanding of how our prejudices and biases influence our interpretations.

For this reason, more interpretations bring out a richer plurality of meanings. (3) The third notion introduced by Gadamer concerns the way that language determines how we experience the world. Gadamer places particular emphasis on the role of language as a foundation for hermeneutics. For him, language is the universal medium of understanding. It is through the conceptual framework of language that we experience the world and share our understanding. There is no experience of the world outside of that shaped by language. For this reason, language is a precondition for understanding. Because we cannot know the world independently of language, our language is said to set limits on our understanding. These limits are set by the manner in which past traditions shape our language and its conceptual representation of the world. For Gadamer, these limits are not a barrier to further understanding. Like prejudices and biases, they represent a starting point for understanding.

Consider the following example of how language sets limits on our understanding. Today we live in the new computer age. Every day we read about the latest technological innovation. However, the language of the computer age continues to rely on the vocabulary of the previous industrial age. Many terms are simple adaptations of concepts from the industrial era—e-mail, telecommuting, chat room, computer, e-commerce. Indeed, technology is moving ahead so swiftly that some terms are made obsolete even as they are being created. The term "on-line" refers to using the Internet with a cable connection. However, today one can be "on-line" via wireless satellite connection. The term is nonsensical. Gadamer would argue that we do not yet have a language for these computer-age phenomena and so we simply impose a vocabulary that reflects our previous understanding of the industrial world. In this way, the language of industrial society sets limits on our understanding of the computer age.

Habermas and the Influence of Social Inequality

The German philosopher Jürgen Habermas takes strong issue with Gadamer. He does so, however, while generally agreeing with Gadamer's criticisms of Dilthey. In *The Logic of the Social Sciences* (1967), Habermas explores the evolution of hermeneutics and concludes with an extended discussion of Gadamer. In essence, he argues that Gadamer does not recognize that the traditions that form an individual's prejudices and biases are, in fact, the product of social practices and institutions that reflect underlying conditions of social inequality. In fact, the purpose of these supposedly benign traditions is to protect and maintain social inequality between groups, such as racial or class disparities. The traditions that arise from conditions of inequality represent ideologies that distort human subjectivity. Habermas's contributions to hermeneutics revolve around, first, his diagnosis of the problem—how ideology is allowed to distort subjectivity—and, second, his remedy—a unique adaptation of psychoanalytical therapy.

(1) Habermas begins by detailing how, he believes, Gadamer allows ideology to distort subjectivity. Gadamer mistakenly treats the prejudices and biases that arise from tradition as somehow representing an individual's pure subjectivity, untainted by historical social conditions such as inequality. Habermas argues that this blinds Gadamer to the ideological nature of human subjectivity. The ideological nature of human subjectivity follows from the fact that a person's understanding of the world can be distorted by popular ideologies that imply that the narrow interests of those in power are, in fact, the universal interests of everyone in society. When those who are not in power unwittingly adopt the interests of those who are in power, Habermas says they are suffering from an alienated consciousness. They are alienated from their own true self-interest.

When asked why he refused to join the U.S. military in Vietnam, Muhammad Ali is said to have responded, "No Vietcong ever called me Nigger." Ali argued that African Americans were oppressed in the United States by those in the dominant white power structure who asked African Americans to fight the Vietnamese. African Americans were not oppressed by Vietnamese people. Therefore, African Americans had interests that were distinct from those of the dominant white power structure in the United States. As a result, African Americans who supported the war in Vietnam were adopting the interests of the dominant white power structure and not their own interests. Ali's remarks suggest that they were alienated from their true self-interest as African Americans. The long-running Uncle Tom stereotype in the United States is based on this premise of alienated consciousness.

To make sense of Habermas's argument, it is again useful to return to the notion of human nature. As noted, for Dilthey, it is the nature of human beings to create meaningful things. For Heidegger and Gadamer, it is the nature of human beings to interpret the meaning of things. Habermas, in effect, sides with Heidegger and Gadamer. However, he adds a critical dimension. It is true that the primary activity of human beings is to interpret the meaning of things in the world around them. And it is true that they do so with the prejudices and biases that are the product of their traditions. However, the immediate understanding that derives from this interpretation does not reflect genuine human subjectivity. Rather, it reflects a human subjectivity that is distorted by ideologies grounded in historical social conditions. This is because all traditions are themselves the products of social practices and institutions that maintain and perpetuate social inequality.

Consider how one might interpret *A Tale of Two Cities* from the perspective of Dilthey, Gadamer, and Habermas. From Dilthey's perspective, the novel is a genuine reflection of Dickens's subjectivity. To fully understand its meaning, it is necessary to become completely absorbed in the life and times of Dickens. Dilthey emphasizes a careful reconstruction of the author's life-world. From Gadamer's perspective, Dilthey offers a semiuseful start. To begin, it must be recognized that a completely objective reconstruction of Dickens's life-world is not possible. There must be an equally rigorous effort to investigate the life and times of the interpreter. Gadamer emphasizes the so-called mediation of horizons, the blending of the subjectivity of the author with that of the interpreter. From Habermas's perspective, there is a further step. It is necessary to analyze the conditions of social inequality that formed the categories of understanding of the author of *A Tale of Two Cities*. These form the unexplored ideology through which Dickens sees the world. Habermas emphasizes the nature of a nineteenth-century, class-divided capitalist society and how it distorted Dickens's own subjectivity and resulted in certain ideological characterizations.

Gadamer had criticized Dilthey for thinking that an interpreter can overcome his or her own subjective position (prejudices and biases) through a systematic reconstruction of past meanings. Habermas similarly criticizes Gadamer for thinking that an interpreter can overcome the fact that conditions of social inequality distort subjective meaning (in the form of ideologies that mask their links to social inequality) through his mediation of horizons. For Gadamer, human subjectivity represents a kind of abstract reasoning that resides in an individual's mind. For Habermas, human subjectivity is the product of an individual's material world that reflects conditions of social inequality.

At best, Habermas argues, Gadamer's approach will indirectly lead to a better understanding of the conditions of social inequality and the ideologies they give rise to. By examining subjectivity in this way, one might better understand that a certain racial group is dominant, that certain religious beliefs and practices prevail, or that a small, wealthy social class is in command. However, one will not learn about genuine individual subjectivity (a person's actual wants and needs). All one discovers is how individual subjectivity reflects a form of alienated consciousness. It is in this sense that people are alienated from their own self-interest and unwittingly adopt a conceptual understanding of the world that furthers the power of the dominant social elites.

(2) Habermas believes that the remedy for ideological distortion can be found in the insights of psychoanalysis. Freedom from the tyranny of tradition (and from alienated consciousness) is only possible if the mediation of horizons referred to by Gadamer takes into account how ideologies distort an individual's understanding of the world. Habermas argues that hermeneutics must both account for the social inequality that gives rise to a distorted understanding and at the same time respect (and liberate) human subjectivity to express itself. To do so, Habermas turns to what he believes to be an analogous process in the realm of Freudian psychoanalysis. Just as the individual seeks to overcome repressed desires in psychoanalysis, humanity must overcome its alienated consciousness.

Sigmund Freud (1856–1939) developed his method of psychoanalysis to better understand how social norms and practices substitute for an individual's repressed wants and needs. Successful psychoanalysis leads patients to a self-conscious realization that they have been repressing certain desires and substituting socially acceptable alternatives for these. A therapist can guide this process, but patients must cure themselves. Habermas argues that hermeneutics can play a similar role to free humanity from its distorted understanding. This requires revealing how conditions of social inequality are at the core of alienated consciousness.

At the level of the individual, one might repress the desire to scream at the boss by developing aggressive driving habits. At the level of humanity, the members of an oppressed social class might repress a subjective desire to live free of the constraints of oppressive social institutions by convincing themselves that they can live lives of fulfillment through conspicuous consumption. Thus, the development of the individual is analogous to the development of humanity. In each case, desires and subjectivity are repressed. For individuals, this results in neurosis. For humanity, it results in ideologies. Psychoanalysis helps individuals recover their repressed desires. Habermas hopes that a modified form of psychoanalysis can also help emancipate humanity from the ideologies that distort understanding. Hermeneutics must be transformed into a guided process of self-reflection—a sustained critique of ideology—that reveals the distorting influence of conditions of social inequality. Habermas referred to this type of hermeneutics as depth hermeneutics.

Dilthey's Defenders

While Gadamer and Habermas debated actively, both are in general agreement that Dilthey's project of reconstructing the life-world of past individuals so as to derive an objective understanding of their subjectivity is without merit. Not everyone agrees with this dour assessment. The Italian legal historian Emilio Betti (1890–1968), for one, argues strenuously that Dilthey's fundamental project of reconstructing the past to establish the original subjective meaning of an actor is indeed a realizable endeavor. In *Hermeneutics as the General Methodology of Geisteswissenschaften* (1962), Betti provides a sweeping synthesis of the hermeneutic tradition. (*Geisteswissenschaften* refers to the cultural and historical sciences pertaining to the study of human beings. It contrasts with *Naturwissenschaften,* or the natural sciences). This is done in an effort to establish the validity of hermeneutics as a source of knowledge in opposition to both Gadamer's attacks and those of positivist critics.

Like Dilthey, Betti believes that the role of the interpreter is to faithfully reconstruct the subjectivity of persons from the past in an effort to understand their original intent. The meaning of any object is dependent upon the subjective purpose of its creator. A similar argument is often attributed to members of the U.S. Supreme Court. Some justices, akin to Gadamer, argue that the U.S. Constitution is a living document whose meaning has evolved over the centuries. Other justices, akin to Betti, argue that any interpretation of the U.S. Constitution must adhere to the original intent of its authors.

The French philosopher Paul Ricoeur (1913–) offers a variation on Betti's rejection of Gadamer. In *Hermeneutics and the Human Sciences* (1981), Ricoeur argues that, rather than aspiring to the positivist ambition of knowledge based on certainty, hermeneutics must strive to produce knowledge based on probability. (A similar point was being made in the context of postpositivist debates at the time.) The goal of hermeneutics is to propose possible interpretations. Eventually, a number of probability judgments are built up and the most convincing interpretation can be selected from a slate of options. In this respect, no interpretation is ever complete or final. The analogy for this process is that of legal arguments in a court of law. Lawyers construct the most plausible explanation for their client based on an interpretation of available evidence and try to persuade a jury that their interpretation is the most convincing.

What Are the Implications of Hermeneutics?

Given the varying approaches to hermeneutics by the authors considered here, precisely identifying broad, unifying themes can be challenging. However, across the competing perspectives, it is possible to find five common premises of hermeneutics that help set it apart from positivism and structuralism. A number of implications follow from each premise.

(1) The first premise concerns a basic distinction between the physical and social sciences based on human subjectivity. The physical sciences investigate inanimate objects void of individual

subjectivity. The social sciences investigate human beings. As such, the interpretation of individual subjectivity plays a central role. It is argued that for scientific inquiry to account for human subjectivity a radical shift is required in methodological assumptions, procedures, and tools. The interpretation of meaning replaces observation and measurement as the fundamental activity of the social sciences. Three implications follow from this.

First, the notion of scientific objectivity must be reconsidered. Proponents of hermeneutics focus on the limitations of objectivity in interpreting human subjectivity. Some proponents reject any hope of objectivity while others detail its limitations. Similar to the arguments of Wittgenstein, it is maintained that there is no such thing as an objective perspective free of prejudice and bias. For some, such as Dilthey, this simply means that one has to remain resolute in accounting for one's biases, with the goal of overcoming them. For others, such as Gadamer, it is not possible to overcome one's prejudices and biases and hope to catch a completely objective glimpse of human subjectivity.

Second, there is greater reliance on probabilistic knowledge (in the social sciences) rather than on certain knowledge (as in the physical sciences). This is because human subjectivity is such that certainty in interpretation is never attainable. In this sense, the rules of evidence are quite different for the physical and social sciences. In the physical sciences, proof is based on securing intersubjective agreement concerning logical deductions and empirical findings. This brings one closer to certain knowledge. In the social sciences of hermeneutics, proof is not the goal at all. Rather, evidence is presented in the form of an argument in which one's interpretation of human subjectivity is compared to another interpretation. This results in probabilistic knowledge.

Third, proponents of hermeneutics maintain that the uncertainty inherent in interpreting human subjectivity results in prioritizing argument and debate (rationalism) over empirical proof in interpreting human subjectivity. This point can be confusing. It is not meant to imply that empiricism is not used in gathering evidence about human subjectivity—for example, examining cultural artifacts from a previous era. It merely implies that there will be a greater reliance on rationalism (over empiricism) in justifying one's interpretation. Notice also that there is a certain overlap between the methodological implications of hermeneutics in this regard and those of postpositivism as discussed in chapter 3.

(2) The second premise of hermeneutics concerns a shift in emphasis away from explanation and toward understanding as the purpose of scientific inquiry. In fact, almost all of the distinctive insights of hermeneutics follow from this shift owing to the fact that its counterpart, positivism, is premised on developing explanations. While most debates within positivism concern how to construct a more accurate explanation of phenomena, the debates within hermeneutics turn on how to construct a more convincing interpretive understanding. Explanation hinges on identifying precise mechanisms that bring about a certain phenomenon. Understanding hinges on interpreting human subjectivity. Three implications follow from this distinction between explanation and understanding.

First, explanations generally contain causal claims. These causal claims are based on identifying a mechanism that is responsible for a specific phenomenon. Within hermeneutics, arguments based on causality are not possible. The emphasis is on probable, rather than necessary, relationships between phenomena. As a consequence, past events are never inevitable. Why a certain event *did not* occur is as important as why an event *did* occur. Second, it follows that the positivist nomothetic approach (based on general laws and deduction) is not a viable approach for hermeneutics. General laws are only of interest to those pursuing explanations of phenomena, not those pursuing understanding. Third, without causation and without an appeal to general laws, there is no basis for the prediction of future events. Prediction, it will be recalled, from the time of Bacon has been a central justification for scientific inquiry based on positivism.

(3) The third premise of hermeneutics concerns the relative nature of competing interpretations. Because there is no absolute standard of truth, two researchers' interpretations of human subjectivity are inherently relative. As a result, hermeneutics unfolds as a formal process of argumentation in which competing interpretations are advanced. When researchers interpret the subjective meaning of past events, they must frame their analysis so as to provide a compelling case that their interpretation is the most convincing. Two implications follow from this.

First, similar to the position taken by some advocates of postpositivism, the ideal of absolute truth is unattainable. At best, one might approximate truth. The result can be a hopeless relativism in which all truths are considered equally valid because there is no absolute standard of truth. However, the more common position within hermeneutics is that the accuracy of an interpretation can be well justified or poorly justified and this is the best measure of its truth. Second, it further follows that the interpretation of an event can never be complete and final. Because any interpretation is based on past interpretations (and current prejudices and biases), any contemporary interpretation is necessarily premised on the fact that there will be future interpretations, which will further develop our understanding.

(4) The fourth premise of hermeneutics concerns the manner in which assumptions about human nature shape how one conducts interpretation. As discussed above, the assumptions of Dilthey, Heidegger, Gadamer, and Habermas about human nature were at the foundation of their conceptual differences. How one character-izes the primary activity of human beings determines where one focuses attention and how one organizes one's analysis of human subjectivity. Therefore, how one defines human nature is crucial. Two implications follow from this.

First, a researcher must explicitly define human nature prior to beginning work. This is because the researcher's notion of human nature provides a set of preliminary assumptions for hermeneutic interpretation. Second, the researcher must remain alert for two dangers related to this point—fundamentalism and relativism. In the case of fundamentalism, the danger is that a researcher will simply construct a vision of human nature and all conclusions will me-chanically follow from this. These conclusions cannot be chal-lenged because they follow from the fundamental premises of what the researcher asserts a human being to be. In the case of relativ-ism, the danger is that a researcher will be forced to acknowledge that his or her conclusions merely follow from an arbitrary set of assumptions regarding human nature and will, therefore, be unable to defend those conclusions beyond this point when confronted by researchers with opposing sets of assumptions regarding human nature.

(5) The fifth premise of hermeneutics concerns the central role of historical and cultural circumstances in shaping subjective mean-ing. There is a certain chicken-and-egg dilemma related to individual

subjectivity and historical and cultural conditions. To what extent do these conditions shape individual subjectivity and to what extent does individual subjectivity shape these conditions? Within hermeneutics, there is a commitment to respecting the autonomy of individual subjectivity. At the same time, there is a continued emphasis on the power of historical and cultural conditions to influence individual subjectivity. Structuralism confronts similar issues and tends to favor the influence of historical and cultural conditions. Hermeneutics, by contrast, tends to favor individual subjectivity. Two implications follow from this dilemma.

First, any hermeneutic interpretation of human subjectivity must be grounded in concrete material conditions. This means that any interpretation requires a detailed description of the historical and cultural conditions from which human subjectivity emerged. Pure, abstract reason—as in phenomenology—is not permissible. There must be an effort to locate individual subjectivity in a specific social context. In this sense, it is impossible to separate individuals' subjectivity from their life-world. There is no such thing as a pure, unadulterated form of individual subjectivity. Second, the life-world of individuals shapes their language of expression. It determines what they know and how they explain what they know. Individuals' life-world—their historical and cultural setting—therefore, determines both their subjectivity and their means of expressing it.

FURTHER READING

Anderson, Robert, John Hughes, and Wesley Sharrock. "Hermeneutics." Pp. 63–82 in *Philosophy and the Human Sciences*. London: Croom Helm, 1986.

Gorner, Paul. "The German Tradition." Pp. 1–16 in *Twentieth Century German Philosophy*. New York: Oxford University Press, 2000.

Martin, Michael. "The Classical *Verstehen* Position." Pp. 7–41 in *Verstehen*. New Brunswick, N.J.: Transaction Publishers, 2000.

Mueller-Vollmer, Kurt. "Language, Mind, and Artifact: An Outline of Hermeneutic Theory Since the Enlightenment." Pp. 1–54 in *The Hermeneutics Reader*. Edited by Kurt Mueller-Vollmer. New York: Continuum Press, 1994.

West, David. "Historicism, Hermeneutics, and Phenomenology." Pp. 79–116 in *An Introduction to Continental Philosophy*. Cambridge, UK: Polity Press, 1996.

6

Antifoundationalism

WHAT IS ANTIFOUNDATIONALISM?

Antifoundationalism refers to a movement tied to a collection of social theorists who are unified less by a common project than by a common critique. This critique concerns how—beginning with the eighteenth-century Enlightenment—Western civilization has been obsessed with (1) the search for foundational knowledge and (2) the role of reason as the source of knowledge and truth. Foundational knowledge implies a set of universal premises that provide a demonstrable basis for certainty and truth. Before the Enlightenment, foundational knowledge was based on church doctrine. In the post-Enlightenment period, foundational knowledge is attributed to reason. To unravel the consequences of this, it is helpful to first consider the general critique offered by antifoundationalism that serves as a response to post-Enlightenment thought.

The Enlightenment opened a new era of hope in the West. At the core of post-Enlightenment optimism is the belief that human reason is capable of dissecting and understanding our world and of prescribing solutions for its progressive development. Post-Enlightenment thought seeks to uncover the essential architecture of the physical and social worlds. By stripping away the thick layers of superstition and tradition that cloud human understanding, post-Enlightenment thinkers are able to tap into a reserve of human reason that provides tools and insights to analyze and ultimately transform their world. This was the hope of the Enlightenment.

Proponents of antifoundationalism today stand aghast as they survey the world built by four centuries of unbridled human reason.

The critique that emerges from this survey is complex and requires a good deal of counterintuitive thinking. To carry out its mission, reason requires a precise road map. This takes the form of large-scale social models. Antifoundationalists argue that efforts to explain complex social processes via these large-scale models (as in the case of structuralism) have produced distortions and fictions—such as the notion of linear, regular patterns of social development. In essence, there is too great a confidence in our ability to systematically understand the dynamics of a society that, in fact, defy formal categories and comprehensive models.

Model-building in the social sciences originates from the post-Enlightenment faith that the methods of the physical sciences are equally applicable in the social world. It is assumed that, just as all physical phenomena can be explained by the right model of nature, all social phenomena can be explained by the right model of the social world. Therefore, human reason is called upon to construct elaborate models of society. These models claim to explain both contemporary social conditions (such as urban poverty) and a society's historical development (such as the transition from agrarian to industrial society).

Because these models are akin to telling the story of social development, they are sometimes referred to as narratives. For example, a theory of why urban schools declined in the late twentieth century would be "a narrative of urban school decline." An assumption of such social models—also borrowed from the physical sciences—is that there is a stable and regular pattern of social development. This development is linear and predictable, so one can chart where a society is within an ongoing process. Proponents of antifoundationalism strongly contest this assumption. For this reason, when analyzing social development, they emphasize periods of discontinuity that disrupt stable patterns or cases that do not conform to a model's linear assumptions.

Within antifoundationalism, the most fundamental social concepts—such as society itself—are in dispute. Proponents of antifoundationalism argue, for example, that the concept of society is far less coherent and ordered than most post-Enlightenment theories would suggest. In fact, how one conceptualizes society is considered largely the invention of theory. The purpose of such an invention is not to advance general knowledge about society but to legitimize (and privilege) a theorist's own knowledge. For example, imagine that you have developed a brilliant new theory of criminal behavior. If you are able to convince the general population of this new theory and new policies emerge based on this, then you have gained a good deal of control and influence through your invented theory.

The legacy of post-Enlightenment thought is the image of an orderly world held together by regular patterns, universal laws, stability, linear progress, common understanding, and predictability based on certainty. The manner in which proponents of antifoundationalism attack each of these, in turn, provides unique insight into the project of antifoundationalism as a critique. Regular patterns are nothing more than self-fulfilling prophecies. They merely follow—all too conveniently—from a contrived set of premises. Universal laws are, in fact, partisan belief systems. They are the inventions of theorists imposing one set of beliefs over another.

Faith in the stability of social phenomena—and in the relationships between phenomena—is a critical anchor for post-Enlightenment thought. This stability is a requirement for having anything meaningful to say about a social system. Upon closer scrutiny, the notion of social stability is considered a convenient contrivance. The norm among social phenomena is dynamic change. Linear progress is an ideology that tries to bring an artificial order to an otherwise chaotic and discontinuous process of development. The idea that there is shared, common understanding across society is pure fiction. This lie conceals the fact that, across society, there is fragmented understanding, corresponding to a plurality of interests. Lastly, predictability and certainty signal human reason's naïve effort to hold together a splintered world of indeterminacy and great uncertainty.

When considering antifoundationalism, it is helpful to keep three caveats in mind. First, antifoundationalism is better thought of as a broad tendency than as a coherent school of thought. There are no overarching, unifying principles or even an agreed-upon project. This makes summary and generalizations all but impossible. Second, antifoundationalism takes the form of a critique. It is not an advocacy of anything in particular; it is more a destruction of everything. This makes the construction of a coherent research program with distinct methods all but impossible. Third, antifoundationalism provides a critique of other critiques and other schools of thought (e.g., structuralism or Marxism). For this reason, to assess most antifoundationalist arguments often requires a good deal of knowledge about prior debates and critiques. Much of antifoundationalist thought is presented in the form of juxtaposition and counterclaims. Given the breadth of issues and authors addressed, presenting a convenient catalog of the positions they attack—as in the case postpositivist responses to logical positivists—is next to impossible.

It is, finally, important to briefly address this chapter's organization and the term "antifoundationalism" itself. The style of presentation throughout this book is notably inconsistent with certain basic principles of antifoundationalism. The chapters are designed to synthesize broad currents within research methods and to reduce complex arguments to their most basic elements. Antifoundationalist writing tends to be fragmentary and purposely nonsystematic. Proponents of antifoundationalism would certainly object to any overarching summary and it is only sensible to acknowledge this obvious contradiction at the start. In addition, the term antifoundationalism warrants brief explanation. Antifoundationalism is, at times, referred to by others as postmodernism. The word postmodernism, however, conjures up different images for different people. Some despise it, others embrace it. For this reason, the more neutral (and literal) term, antifoundationalism, has been adopted here.

WHAT ARE THE ORIGINS OF ANTIFOUNDATIONALISM?

The origins of antifoundationalism can be traced to three sources: the work of Friedrich Nietzsche (1844–1900), the conceptualizations of modernity and rationalization, and post–World War II French social theory. The influence of Nietzsche is difficult to exaggerate. His work occupies a central role for almost all antifoundationalist writers. Three themes are of particular importance. First is Nietzsche's extreme skepticism, which took the form of sustained nihilism. (Nihilism is an extreme form of skepticism that rejects any claims for an objective basis for truth.) The result has been a profound questioning of any truth claims. Nietzsche's rejection of literal meaning led him to treat all language as metaphorical. In this sense, the meaning of what one says is never straightforward. Lastly, Nietzsche's belief that knowledge claims are thinly disguised efforts to legitimize one belief system over another has been characterized as the "will-to-power." The search for truth is usurped by the drive for power.

Modernity and rationalization provide the scenic backdrop for the antifoundationalist critique of post-Enlightenment thought. Modernity was the name given to a range of new social and political institutions linked to democracy and capitalism beginning in sixteenth-century Europe. Rationalization was the tool by which erratic and unpredictable social institutions and practices were made uniform and consistent across society. Today, modernity and rationalization are the minimal prerequisites to be considered an enlightened modern society. The influence of French social theory is fairly self-evident. In the post–World War II era, the principal proponents of antifoundationalism have been French. There are two factors to consider here. On the one hand, at the end of World War II the dominant social theories in France were structuralism and Marxism—two of the main targets of antifoundationalism. On the other hand, beginning in the 1940s, French society underwent a series of socially jarring and culturally disruptive changes, as a vibrant, new, urban-industrial lifestyle supplanted France's traditional agrarian roots. French antifoundationalists insisted that the inherited social theory was outdated and could not adequately account for post–World War II developments.

Friedrich Nietzsche

The German philosopher Friedrich Nietzsche is a central figure in the development of antifoundationalism. Nietzsche was a harsh critic of post-Enlightenment beliefs. These views are explored in a number of his works such as *Birth of Tragedy* (1872), *Thus Spoke Zarathustra* (1885), and *Genealogy of Morals* (1887). However, in keeping with his belief that broad, sweeping generalizations should be avoided, Nietzsche organized his thoughts in a series of brief books. He does not attempt to provide a comprehensive summary of his thoughts, so it is necessary to pull the key ideas driving his work from this collection of extended essays.

Proponents of antifoundationalism have adopted from Nietzsche three themes in particular. (1) The first concerns nihilism—his extreme skepticism toward truth claims—and the related claim that God is dead. The target of Nietzsche's nihilism is the post-Enlightenment notion of reason itself and the truths it claims to uncover. He argues that these truths are, in fact, nothing more than the beliefs and opinions of various people. The systems of reason (such as positivism) that developed during the post-Enlightenment period are merely systems of persuasion. Nietzsche set out to expose these untruths for what they truly are. He concludes that there is no one reality to consider. There are many realities.

For human reason to explain the world it must first impose an order on the world. Imposing an order on the world involves constructing a reality that describes the world. It is this notion of reality—an artificial construct of human reason, in his view—that Nietzsche rejects. This, in turn, ushers in hopeless uncertainty. Nietzsche believes that we are all resigned to this uncertainty and, for this reason, he says that God is dead. Appealing to God as the architect of the world brought certainty and order. There is no such certainty and order and so there is no God (in the Judeo-Christian sense of a deity). As also argued by certain proponents of hermeneutics, Nietzsche concludes that there are no facts, only interpretations. This is what is meant by many realities.

(2) This notion of uncertainty and the absence of any single, fixed reality points to a second contention of Nietzsche regarding the role of metaphors in explanations or descriptions of the world. The goal of much scientific inquiry is to develop a language that can describe the world literally. The premise of such an effort is that—whatever the differences regarding our understanding of the world—at least we can share a common language that describes the same underlying reality in the world. For Nietzsche there is no such shared, underlying reality, only various interpretations of reality. Therefore, the goal of a literal language corresponding to a single, fixed reality is pure illusion.

Instead, Nietzsche argues that explanations and descriptions of the world rely on overlapping metaphors that reflect a particular interpretation of reality. In this sense, a metaphor serves as convenient shorthand for presenting the world through familiar images. The Scottish political economist Adam Smith (1723–1790) relied on the metaphor of the marketplace to describe society. The British sociologist Herbert Spencer (1820–1903) borrowed metaphors from

the field of biology. Nietzsche suggests that exploring such metaphors will expose the underlying assumptions of a theorist's interpretation. In the case of Smith, there is an assumption that the
division of labor shapes the social order. In the case of Spencer,
there is an assumption that social development follows an evolutionary pattern.

Importantly, the use of metaphors is not an addition to language. It is not a colorful embellishment. It is an essential and
necessary part of language that cannot be avoided. In other words,
all we have are metaphors to express ourselves. We operate with
metaphors that reflect our perspective. This imposes certain limitations on the use of language. For instance, if all language is limited
by one's perspective, then how can one critically engage one's own
perspectives' biases? Nietzsche's response is important because it is
reflected across a good deal of antifoundationalist writing. He suggests that one must deliberately reverse the metaphors reflecting
one's perspective. In other words, one must purposely invert the
meaning of the assumptions lodged within one's perspective so as
to undo the prioritization they have been given.

(3) The third important theme taken from Nietzsche concerns
the so-called will-to-power and the role of instrumental reason. The
will-to-power is an extension of the implications of nihilism and
multiple realities. While Nietzsche argues that there are multiple
realities (and multiple ways to impose order on the world), he does
not believe that such realities are arbitrary in origin. Various realities (or truths) correspond with various interests of social groups. In
this manner, truth is used to privilege one group above another.
The application of reason is, therefore, never neutral. It serves
specific ends.

When reason serves the purpose of certain social groups, the
interests of those social groups will determine truth. Under these
circumstances, an inevitable power struggle emerges—one social
class versus another, one religious community versus another, or
the developed world versus the underdeveloped world. The will-
to-power represents the struggle between social groups to have
their truths recognized and validated. Nietzsche takes this a step
further and argues that, beyond simple truth and error, all of the
basic dualities of the post-Enlightenment period—good and evil,
free and unfree, sane and insane—are reflections, not of real

differences, but of groups jockeying for social power. As a consequence, there is no one inherent definition of what is true and what is false or what is good and what is evil.

Modernity and Rationalization

The twin images of modernization and rationalization emerge in the post-Enlightenment period as central to the application of human reason to the organization of society. The term modernity is not precisely defined nor can it be given specific dates. Most generically, modernity represents a period in the development of Western civilization beginning sometime in the sixteenth century. For some, modernity continues to this day. For others, we are in a period of transition—hence, the term postmodernity. Modernity is characterized by a constellation of sociocultural, political, and economic developments. The list is long and much contested. It includes the transition from agrarian to industrial society, the replacement of production for local consumption with production for regional markets, the shift from the rule of monarchies to representative democracies, the move from inherited social privilege to free competition for jobs and positions, the replacement of church authority by secular authority. In short, modernity encompasses a broad range of social and political institutions and practices that emerged in the post-Enlightenment period to organize and integrate complex social practices across society.

At the core of modernity is rationalization. Prior to modernity, the primary organizing principles for society were tradition and custom. As a result, great inefficiencies and inequities abounded and people were basically locked into the social position they happened to be born into. To counter this, modernity called upon human reason to emancipate society from the tyranny of tradition and custom. The organization of a modern, free society is orderly and planned. The use of human reason to better organize a social institution (such as the military, the transportation system, or the banking system) is referred to as rationalization. Precise and uniform rules and procedures dictate social interaction in different settings.

Proponents of antifoundationalism argue that modernity yields a peculiar form of freedom. It is suggested that post-Enlightenment modernity began as a movement to emancipate people from the tyranny of custom and tradition. Ultimately, however, the result is a new form of tyranny. The consequence of modernity and rationalization has been the emergence of complex social institutions and practices that represent a mindless subservience to human reason. Rules and stringent regulations, rather than free, independent thought and action, guide and constrain human beings in a modern society. People have broken the chains of custom and tradition only to find themselves locked in the iron cage of the rational, modern world. Proponents of antifoundationalism dedicate their energies to exposing the tyranny of human reason in the modern world.

The French Influence

From the start, French social theory has been at the forefront of antifoundationalist thought. Two factors account for the emergence of antifoundationalist thought in France at the end of World War II. On the one hand, French society underwent a series of intense, large-scale sociocultural changes in a relatively brief period following the war. The immense disruption of traditional, agrarian French society forced social theorists to rethink many of their fundamental assumptions regarding the nature of society and of social change. At the same time, there were distinct intellectual traditions that dominated French social theory in the early twentieth century. These traditions (in part the legacy of Auguste Comte and Emile Durkheim) emphasized a form of social analysis that constructed elaborate models of society featuring universal laws of interaction and development.

Prior to World War II, France was a largely agrarian society. The rapid shift from an agrarian-based society to an urban-industrial society imposed radical new lifestyles and social practices directly on top of centuries-old customs and traditions. There was a general recognition that a new type of society was emerging. However, the social theories on hand proved inadequate to explain the burgeoning mass culture and consumer society that were driven by industrialization and new communication and transportation technologies. As it turned out, the chaos of sudden social change, alongside the impotence of modernist theories to account for these changes, provided the perfect breeding ground for antifoundationalist ideas.

In the mid–twentieth century, French social thought was dominated by structuralism and Marxism. Each of these was premised upon a fixed and predictable image of the world—logical patterns of interaction in the case of structuralism and regular patterns of orderly development in the case of Marxism. Structuralism provided a model of society in which each social phenomenon could be explained as part of a larger social system that was organized around regular patterns of functional interaction. Marxism provided a model of society in which history unfolded as a linear process tied to specific stages of development (from primitive to advanced) that were driven by distinct forms of class conflict at each stage.

The terminology developed by proponents of antifoundationalism in their attack on structuralism and Marxism plays a central role in the development of antifoundationalism. Each is accused of creating "totalizing discourses" that are "closed." The term discourse refers to the use of language within a belief system in a manner that reflects the (hidden) assumptions of that belief system. For example, the authors of the U.S. Constitution developed a discourse about freedom. The belief system of these authors, however, does not apply the same standards of freedom for women and African Americans as for white adult males. Their discourse on freedom (the language they used to discuss freedom) reveals these assumptions of their belief system.

A totalizing discourse is one that usurps all other discourses (and all other belief systems). It presumes that its beliefs and assumptions about the world (and the model of the world that results from these) are the only correct ones. For this reason it is considered closed. Furthermore, the claims and implications of the totalizing discourses associated with structuralism and Marxism are so broad and so encompassing that all social phenomena are explained by these models. Such models posit universal laws from which all else follows. For example, within certain versions of structural-functionalism it is believed that all social phenomena exist to fulfill the specific social purpose of assuring harmony and balance in the social system. It follows that the purpose of any social phenomenon can be explained by demonstrating how it promotes harmony and balance. This is a totalizing discourse insofar as it precludes the possibility of nonharmonious aspects of society such as inherent social conflict.

What Are the Main Elements of Antifoundationalism?

As mentioned, there are many challenges to capturing a sense of antifoundationalism in convenient, summary form. Here, our task is to try to lift out several overriding themes that are common—though not uniformly adopted—across antifoundationalist thought. For this purpose, the discussion is organized around four key topics: (1) post-structuralism, (2) deconstruction, (3) knowledge as narrative, and (4) discontinuities and ruptures. Post-structuralism—through its critique of structural linguistics—has had a central influence on the conceptualizations and terminology of antifoundationalism. Many proponents of antifoundationalism use a form of linguistic analysis known as deconstruction to highlight the hidden assumptions and biases behind an author's (or speaker's) thoughts.

The antifoundationalist notion that all knowledge necessarily takes the form of a narrative points to how certain perspectives are legitimized and others marginalized in society. Whereas traditional historical accounts present social development as a linear, evolutionary process of progress and growth, proponents of antifoundationalism argue that the notion of such neat, schematic histories is a fiction that distorts actual events. They emphasize discontinuities and ruptures in history to highlight these distortions. Importantly, at the core of many antifoundationalist writers' work is an analysis of the relationship between knowledge and power. This concerns both who decides what constitutes knowledge and how a society legitimates the use of knowledge in the exercise of power.

Post-structuralism contra Structural Linguistics

While little time is actually spent defining what is meant by it, a great deal of antifoundationalist thought presumes a familiarity with something called post-structuralism. As one might suspect, post-structuralism is a response to structuralism (see chapter 4). From the post-structuralist perspective, structuralism has two chief defects. First, post-structuralists argue that to treat the structures uncovered by structuralism as timeless and universal explanations of the social world is pure ideology. They maintain that these structures are historical (and not universal) and that they change over time precisely because of the highly dynamic (and unfixed) nature

of society. Second, structuralism's explicit dismissal of human subjectivity results in an overly mechanical interpretation of society.
Within structuralism, an individual's actions and thoughts are ultimately the by-products of structural conditions. Therefore, there is
no realm of individual autonomy or independence from the fixed
laws of structural determinism. Post-structuralists maintain that the
dynamic nature of society is precisely attributable to the contributions of subjective human thoughts and actions.

Proponents of antifoundationalism concentrate heavily on the de-
cisive role of language in shaping social reality. In this respect, post-
structuralism places great emphasis on a critique of structural linguistics.
It will be recalled that the project of structural linguistics—in the
tradition of Ferdinand de Saussure—is to map out a coherent conceptual framework and structure of rules that govern the use of language.
Post-structuralism borrows generously from the conceptualizations and
the language of structural linguistics, for this reason.

The analysis of structural linguistics begins with the relationship
between signifiers and the signified. (As discussed in chapter 4, a
signifier is a sound or symbol that refers to the signified, which is
some thing or concept in the world. For example, the sound "bird"
is associated with a small animal that flies.) Structural linguistics
treats the relationship between signifiers and signified as fixed and
stable within language. If this is correct, then the task of accurately
deciphering meaning is a simple matter of systematically charting
these relationships across a given language. Furthermore, because
the relationship between signifiers and signified (how people use
language to express their world) is universal and unchanging across
a society, one can always determine the meaning of any sentiment
no matter who the speaker is.

Proponents of post-structuralism argue that there is no such
shared, universal meaning that guarantees that one person's use of
language will have the same meaning as another's. At best, one can
argue that there are communities of speakers with shared language
patterns. Prison guards use language differently than elementary
school teachers. But even this breaks down. For example, it is
likely that the way a prison guard from the countryside uses language will have more in common with the language use of a
schoolteacher who is also from the countryside than with that of a
prison guard who is from the city. For post-structuralists, the point

is that there are no fixed and stable relationships between signifiers and signified. The relationship is an arbitrary social convention that is constantly changing and shifting.

Post-structuralism adopts the practice from structural linguistics of analyzing society in terms of signs, symbols, and codes. However, post-structuralism begins with a strategic inversion of a basic premise of structural linguistics. Structural linguistics starts with the signified (the world of social phenomena) and asks how language reflects this world. The signifiers are fixed and stable because the world that is signified is a stable collection of objective things. Post-structuralism begins with the signifier (the social convention supposedly describing the world) and asks how this use of language is shaped by our understanding of the world. The signifier is not fixed and stable because our understanding of the world is not fixed and stable. For example, one of the most essential concepts for U.S. law is that of "citizen." One might think that so crucial a term would have a relatively stable and consistent meaning. However, if one looks back over U.S. history, it is clear that the concept of citizen has radically changed to include categories of people previously excluded, such as former slaves, women, and certain immigrant groups.

Deconstruction and the Perils of Logocentrism

One of the strategies of antifoundationalism is referred to as deconstruction. This involves a concerted effort to expose the embedded (and hidden) meanings and assumptions within our uses of language—primarily speaking and writing. This approach has much in common with Nietzsche's treatment of metaphors and is closely associated with the French philosopher Jacques Derrida. Like Nietzsche, Derrida adopts a writing style that defies general summary or neat synthesis. As a result, his ideas are explored in a number of smaller works, including *Writing and Difference* (1967) and *Of Grammatology* (1967). For Derrida, confusion clouds much work in the social sciences owing to the inherent distortions tied to how we use language to represent social reality.

He shares the view of post-structuralism that there is no direct correspondence between the meaning of a word and what it is supposed to represent in the world. Derrida traces this confusion to the mistaken assumption that true meaning is most fully revealed in those uses of language that are considered to be "present." This mistaken assumption is referred to as logocentrism. The use of the word "present" has a double meaning here. In one sense, something is present if it is physically before us—it is here. In another sense, something is present if it is an occurrence at this specific moment in time—it is now. Derrida relies on both meanings when he refers to "absence," which is the opposite of present (the opposite of something being here and now).

Derrida's argument is actually quite simple. When I speak, my words are said to be present. However, I cannot say anything in the present unless I use words and expressions that derive their meaning from past uses of such words and expressions. For example, if in making my point I refer to the Monroe Doctrine, this will only have meaning if someone is already familiar with this term. Therefore, the notion that, when I speak, my words are "present" and the past words and expressions (which give my words meaning) are "absent" is an illusion. My present words and expressions are dependent upon the so-called absent words and expressions.

However, there is a long post-Enlightenment tradition of treating spoken words as more genuine than written words. This specific manifestation of logocentrism is referred to as phonocentrism. The idea is that when we speak, we somehow have direct, unfiltered access to our thoughts. Post-Enlightenment thought is obsessed with the search for original, unmediated meaning that can provide a completely certain foundation for truth. This is sought in the immediate present for the simple reason that, while we can never be certain about something from the past or in the future, it is assumed that our knowledge of the present can achieve certainty (and authenticity) as we experience it. Derrida flatly rejects the notion that we have any greater access to a completely unmediated present than we do to the past or future. Consequently, he denies any possibility for a completely certain foundation for truth.

Three consequences follow from Derrida's rejection of logocentrism. First, our use of language does not provide direct insight into pure thought. If the words and expressions we use to describe the world derive their meaning from other prior uses of these same words and expressions, then our descriptions are necessarily filtered through other people's thoughts. Second, related to this first point, any use of language is always the continuation of other language uses. Our language derives from social interaction. We are constantly adding to and extending an ongoing process of language formation. Third, no one can claim control over the interpretation of his or her own words. No one can impose his or her own meaning on a text because we all rely upon words and expressions that belong to society in general.

Deconstruction emerges, in part, from Derrida's desire to address the distortions of logocentrism in our use of language. Deconstruction combines several basic strategies for analyzing how language is used in a variety of forms. In fact, Derrida believes that deconstruction is appropriate for any use of language that claims to capture the lived experience of people. Along with standard works in the social sciences, this would therefore include films, music, news, or literature. Within the social sciences, Derrida believes, deconstruction serves as an effective method for exposing the underlying ideological assumptions that organize research methods.

A central task of deconstruction is to demonstrate the fundamental indeterminacy of meaning within language. It is important to break from the assumption that there is a literal connection between words and reality or between the spoken word and the unfiltered mind. As a result, a close reading of any use of language reveals a collection of terms and assumptions that turn out to be contradictory and without foundation. There is a glaring contradiction, for example, in U.S. popular culture between praise for the work ethic and celebrations of those who get something for nothing. On the one hand, there is a deeply ingrained faith in an honest day's pay and patiently reaping what one sows. On the other hand, U.S. society is saturated with news of the latest miracle diet, instant-pay lotteries, and stock market speculation—things that attest to a cultural worship of immediate gratification and effortless gain.

At the heart of deconstruction is the identification of a primary argument that relies upon some claims of foundational truth. Based on this primary argument, a chain of further claims follows. Derrida argues that, in fact, the only way to make a claim is by contrasting something with what it is not. These claims form a string of binary oppositions (such as good/evil, rational/nonrational, sane/insane). Thus, a central task of deconstruction is to examine the chain of claims and the use of binary oppositions that follow from these.

Derrida considers these oppositions to be false dichotomies. By exposing the reliance of an argument on a set of dubious binary oppositions, he hopes to collapse the argument itself. Because binary oppositions contain a hierarchy of values—what is valued, what is disparaged—it is not sufficient to merely identify them within language. As in the case of Nietzsche's treatment of metaphors, the binary oppositions must be inverted and replaced in an effort to delegitimize the hierarchy.

Consider the example of those who support the death penalty for murderers. The central argument is that persons who commit murder should be punished as harshly as possible. Several claims follow from this. Persons who murder are immoral. Persons who murder persons who murder are moral. Persons capable of murder are evil. Persons capable of murdering a person who murders are good. The justice system convicts a person who is guilty. The justice system does not convict a person who is innocent. It is just to murder a person convicted of murder. It is unjust to not murder a person convicted of murder. Some of the binary oppositions that follow from these claims include moral/immoral, good/evil, innocent/guilty, and just/unjust. Derrida asks us to consider the consistency of these binary oppositions and suggests that there is an arbitrariness and a self-serving aspect to how these juxtapositions are framed and presented. In the end, they tell us more about the values associated with the preordained conclusion (murderers should get the death penalty) than about the truth of the central argument.

Knowledge as Narrative

The concept of narrative is a common theme among proponents of antifoundationalism. Narratives operate as frameworks of beliefs that legitimize and organize social institutions and practices (political, religious, economic) by defining the rules of interaction and setting the criteria for judgments. The critique of narratives is explored by the French sociologist Jean-François Lyotard (1924–1998) in *The Postmodern Condition* (1979). Any explanation of social phenomena is, by definition, a narrative. The term narrative is invoked, in part, to suggest storytelling. In other words, an explanation is a form of storytelling. But, of course, there are many other possible stories to tell. So each narrative is only one story (or interpretation).

It is argued that any reasonable effort to explain something will reveal certain insights. However, this will be at the cost of obscuring other insights. For example, imagine that one constructs an explanation (a narrative) of the U.S. civil rights movement in which it is argued that its success was due to strong leadership. This approach will obscure the role of many women behind the scenes who coordinated and organized events while male leaders stood before the microphones. Certain insights regarding the U.S. civil rights movement can be revealed by a focus on male leadership. However, other insights (the critical role of women) are obscured. This doesn't necessarily invalidate a specific narrative. It is simply incomplete—one story among many.

There are many narratives in society. One narrative of democracy legitimizes the political order. One narrative of religion shapes spiritual beliefs. One narrative of justice validates the legal system. (Arguably, there is a significant overlap between the concept of narrative and Wittgenstein's notion of language game from chapter 3.) A critical narrative for any society concerns the production of knowledge and the definition of truth. One of the distinguishing features of a modern society is its replacement of traditional forms of knowledge (superstition, religion, metaphysics) with the narrative of positivist science as the primary source of knowledge.

The manner in which the positivist sciences put forward knowledge claims can be treated as a form of narrative. Lyotard argues that narratives within the positivist sciences exhibit five unique features. First, science is based on a set of standardized and systematic procedures designed to provide verification (or refutation). So scientific knowledge is based on a form of proof. Second, this proof must be supported by a consensus within the scientific community. It must survive the skepticism of the scientist's own peers. Third, scientific knowledge requires the ongoing training of new generations of knowledge producers. Science can only survive as a narrative if the current generation of scientists trains the next generation in the same doctrines of truth (its techniques and ideology). Fourth, scientific knowledge requires the denial of knowledge developed by other narratives. Those societies that do not accept scientific knowledge as the principal source of truth are considered primitive or backward. Fifth, within the positivist science narrative, the production of knowledge is an end in itself. The purpose is to simply reveal the truth.

With the advance of technology in society, Lyotard maintains, there is a crucial shift in the narrative of science. Science shifts from a single, truth-seeking metanarrative to a variety of narrow special-interest narratives. Unlike scientific knowledge, which seeks knowledge for its own sake, technological knowledge seeks knowledge as a means to an end. It follows that a range of scientific-technological narratives emerge, corresponding with various technical applications of knowledge—rather than the single pursuit of universal truth. The goal of science is truth. The goal of technology is efficiency. Furthermore, technology-based science requires equipment and money. Consequently, those with the most money stand the best chance of being judged correct according to the criteria of technology-based science. The purpose of science is no longer to find truth. The new purpose of science and technology is to advance the power and interests of social elites.

The consequences of this shift from a single, pure science narrative to multiple scientific-technological narratives are devastating for those who wish to sustain the superiority of the positivist science narrative over other narratives (or of truth claims in modern societies over those of traditional societies). As science moves from a single, truth-seeking metanarrative, its claims over other nonscientific narratives weaken. The overlapping, nonhierarchical knowledge claims of traditional societies begin to resemble the overlapping, nonhierarchical knowledge claims of advanced technological societies. In addition, the authority of the objective scientist is eroded by the role of wealth in generating knowledge. Within the positivist science narrative, a community of objective scientists produces universal truths. Within scientific-technological narratives, social elites sponsor communities of scientists to produce narrowly applicable knowledge. In traditional societies, those occupying positions of inherited social status (such as shamans or elders) determine truth. In advanced technological societies, those with wealth determine truth.

Discontinuities and Ruptures

A prolific contributor to antifoundationalist thought was the French philosopher Michel Foucault (1926–1984). Of particular interest is Foucault's treatment of discontinuities and ruptures in history. Foucault contrasts his style of writing history (and his emphasis on nonlinear, nonevolutionary development) with traditional approaches that stress the role of universal laws driving linear development. His explicit goal is to historicize and localize what is considered permanent and immutable. A variety of issues related to this approach are explored in many of Foucault's works, including *The Birth of the Clinic* (1963), *The Order of Things* (1966), and *Discipline and Punish* (1975).

Foucault's emphasis on discontinuity and rupture contrasts sharply with the way traditional history is written. Traditional history attempts to place past events within a grand explanatory schema. An example of such a schema would be structuralism. Within grand explanatory schemas there is a linear, logical order that accounts for an event. Related to this, there is a tendency within traditional history to focus on a search for the origin of a given event. The origin of a given event then provides a rationale for the depiction of all historical events based on that assumed origin. For example, those who share the perspective of the Confederacy regarding the U.S. Civil War argue that the war's central issue was the defense of states' rights. From this perspective, one's depiction of the U.S. Civil War—the exact same events and personalities—will differ radically from that of those who believe that slavery was the central issue.

Foucault contrasts the traditional treatment of history with his approach, which he calls genealogical history. While the traditional approach emphasizes continuity and transition, Foucault emphasizes discontinuity and rupture. There is no grand explanatory schema that can account for all events in history. Rather, history unfolds in detached, localized moments. The effort to incorporate historical events into a neat causal chain distorts our understanding of the events and imposes a contrived logic on historical development. Very simply, if you believe that the history of U.S. intervention in Latin America is the story of aggression and exploitation, then you will read this into specific historical events and try to fit them into your model. Likewise, if you believe that the history of U.S. intervention in Latin America is the story of charitable U.S. efforts to help those societies, then, again, you will present events in a manner that fits your assumptions.

Foucault's primary aim is to highlight discontinuity and rupture to reveal the emptiness and artificiality of traditional attempts to construct grand explanatory schemas. He wants to understand what is unique and singular about historical events, rather than how they might conform to a preset formula. He rejects the notion that there are constants or essences driving an inevitable history. He tries to portray histories that are ignored and marginalized by traditional history. These histories represent a rupture in the sense that they do not fit neatly into the grand explanatory schemas. By focusing on the mundane rather than the spectacular he hopes to bring out the local and ordinary nature of historical events that occur beneath the surface. Traditional history tells the history—or presents the perspective—of monarchs and conquerors. Foucault wants to hear the story of the royal subject and the conquered. For this reason, he concentrates on the history of marginalized populations far removed from power—for example, mental patients and prisoners.

In the end, Foucault argues that there are no universal laws governing historical development and, by implication, no encompassing theories capable of explaining it. Rather, by focusing on discontinuities and ruptures, he attempts to demonstrate that true history is a series of nonevolutionary and fragmentary developments. These represent moments of development with no causal chains and no precise origins. It is not that there are no connections between events in history. It is merely that by imposing one set of assumptions regarding historical explanation, one automatically precludes a whole series of counterassumptions. Each set of assumptions emphasizes and gives voice to one set of people while silencing another group. One's choice of assumptions, therefore, comes with severe consequences.

WHAT ARE THE IMPLICATIONS OF ANTIFOUNDATIONALISM?

As discussed earlier, antifoundationalism does not lend itself to broad, sweeping generalizations. Antifoundationalism represents a critique of scientific inquiry rather than a coherent program of study. It is necessary, therefore, to pull out certain issues and themes that are largely applicable across this critique, though they cannot necessarily be associated with all proponents of antifoundationalism. In this regard, there are five premises to consider. A number of specific implications follow from each.

(1) The first premise of antifoundationalism asserts that there is no certain knowledge. The notion here is not simply that certain knowledge is difficult—or virtually impossible—to obtain. Many others, such as postpositivists, argue that absolute certainty is a noble aspiration that is simply beyond our limited grasp. Proponents of antifoundationalism reject even the aspiration. This is because the pursuit of certain knowledge is portrayed as a strategy to control and manipulate others—the will-to-power. Thus, the argument against certain knowledge is an argument (a) that all knowledge claims are true only in relation to a particular perspective and (b) that knowledge claims always imply power grabs in which one positions oneself to gain advantage over others.

Two implications follow from this. First, as others have argued, all knowledge claims are, in fact, merely interpretations that reflect an individual's social background and interests. Objective truth is a myth that serves the narrow interests of those proclaiming it. Second, there is no one reality. We are always operating within a mix of realities for the simple reason that we are always exposed to contending perspectives. When twenty people watch a movie, it is not that there are twenty distinct experiences of a single reality on the screen. Rather, the reality on the screen is determined by how each person experiences that movie. That all viewers may have literally seen the same sequence of visual images does not mean that they have all interpreted these images in precisely the same way, as a single, common reality. Moreover, were the same twenty persons to watch the same movie once more, it is likely that they will experience it differently than the first time. Images will have different meanings. There is no one reality because the way reality is shaped is undergoing constant change.

(2) The second premise of antifoundationalism emphasizes the role of open explanations. The use of open explanations recognizes the fact that history—and our knowledge of it—is never complete. All arguments must be offered as reasonable interpretations open to revision. Reliance on definitive conclusions denies the fact, not merely that one might be wrong, but that one might be only temporarily correct. In other words, there must be a recognition (a) that all truths are open to being wrong and (b) that all truths are open to being accurate today and inaccurate tomorrow. The argument that the truth of any knowledge claim can change over time

automatically precludes the use of any closed explanations. (And, yes, whether this claim is itself subject to later revision is an open question.)

Two implications follow from this. First, there is a strong bias against any form of model-building. The role of models within an explanation is to suggest the inevitability of certain outcomes. A social science model is a structural template that attempts to explain historical events or social developments. Proponents of antifoundationalism are not as concerned with the elimination of subjective autonomy—as stressed by hermeneutics—as they are with the mechanical rationale behind model-building. Models lead to closed interpretations of reality that fit within a narrow range of options as determined by the model's assumptions. When a person's conclusions simply follow from a firm set of prior assumptions, there is little need for any actual investigation.

Second, proponents of antifoundationalism mount a ferocious opposition to any closed narratives, in connection with model-building or otherwise. Closed narratives usually take the form of grand theory. The argument here is similar to that related to model-building. Closed narratives are elaborate explanations that take the form of structural theories based on logical mechanisms of development and sets of categories by which to classify social phenomena. Logical mechanisms tell us why certain things happened. Categories tell us how to interpret phenomena. Both of these limit our understanding by limiting our perspective and by closing off alternative explanations. A closed narrative is not presented as one interpretation among many. It is presented as the most accurate interpretation available.

(3) The third premise of antifoundationalism concerns the role of metaphors within our language of explanation. The basic argument is that it is impossible to speak without metaphors. A metaphor operates as a type of road sign or landmark that helps us navigate our way. In this way, metaphors provide both an imagery of how one sees the world and a language for expressing this image. Comte believed that society could be understood by comparing it to a biological organism. For example, the human body has been described as a set of structures with an ascending order of complexity—cells, tissues, organs, subsystems of organs, the complete organism. Comte describes society in a corresponding

fashion. Thus, tissues (the family unit) are made of cells (individuals). Organs (communities) are made of tissues (families). Organs (communities) are linked to create subsystems (e.g., religions, the economic system). The full organism (society) is the combination of subsystems. In this manner, the metaphor shapes how one describes and explains social phenomena.

There are two implications based on this. First, it is argued that there can be no literal meaning within language. There is no direct correspondence between a word and the phenomenon to which it refers. Rather, all words are filtered through conceptual metaphors. Harriet Tubman's "underground railroad" is an example. The term underground railroad is not a literal description of the transportation of slaves from the U.S. South to the North. However, it suggests an imagery that helps one to understand and conceptualize how the transportation of slaves operated. Logical empiricism attempts to construct a precise language that corresponds directly with observable phenomena. Proponents of antifoundationalism, along with many postpositivists, deny that this is possible. Postpositivists maintain that this is impossible because methods of observation are always theory laden (see chapter 3). Proponents of antifoundationalism maintain that this is impossible owing to the intrinsic role of metaphors in our language of explanation. Metaphoric language reflects how we see and understand the world.

Second, the meaning of a person's own words (the words of either a speaker or a writer) is not for the person to decide. Meaning is socially determined. This has two aspects to it. On the one hand, the meaning of a person's words is defined by past usage. All of the words, phrases, and images that one uses in everyday language are the fossils of previous generations of speakers and writers. Each is coded with a common social understanding prior to any contemporary use. On the other hand, the meaning of a person's words is subject to contemporary social standards. There are rules and commonly understood uses of language in any society. If one stays within these rules, the meaning of one's words will be interpreted within accepted community norms of meaning. If one goes outside these rules, one's words will likely have no meaning. Proponents of antifoundationalism, therefore, deny speakers and writers the sole right to interpret what they mistakenly believe to be their own words.

(4) The fourth premise of antifoundationalism maintains that social phenomena are in a constant state of flux. Their form and substance are ever changing. It is difficult to define, classify, and explain a given phenomenon because its characteristics and its relationships to other phenomena are constantly shifting. For this reason there is a need to constantly reexamine one's basic assumptions and to challenge notions of permanent, unchanging conditions. For example, the role of public education in the United States has undergone major changes over the past century. In the 1920s, public education was a vehicle for developing citizenship skills in new immigrants. During the Cold War, it was a matter of national defense. It stressed math and science in an effort to keep up with the Soviet Union after the launch of *Sputnik.* In the 1980s, providing future workers with basic computational and literacy skills was emphasized. Still, people discuss public education as though it were some timeless, unchanging entity—as in the idea that we need to "get back to basics."

Two implications follow from the idea that social phenomena are in constant flux. First, it naturally follows that it is not possible to assign a fixed and permanent meaning to a specific phenomenon. This is demonstrated by the previous example of public education. The meaning attached to any phenomenon will change over time and it is incorrect to refer to an item's true nature or most basic qualities. In general, social research is based on the presumption that the meaning of social phenomena is fixed and permanent. This is the basis for making comparisons within the social sciences. Without the ability to draw comparisons, we are stuck with little more than a series of temporary, descriptive vignettes.

Second, one cannot premise analysis on a stable set of relationships between social phenomena. This, however, is a basic requirement for nomothetic research. The dependent variable is isolated while tracking changes in the independent variables. Once a relationship is observed between the dependent and independent variables, it is assumed that the relationship applies across all cases. Proponents of antifoundationalism reject this notion of a direct relationship between phenomena in a static condition, held motionless in time. As a result, generalizations—which form the backbone of most of the social sciences—are suddenly no longer possible. We have only the details of individual cases to consider.

(5) The fifth premise of antifoundationalism concerns the role of discontinuity in history. This should not be understood simply as a flat denial of the possibility of continuous, orderly development. More importantly, it is an argument that by examining periods of discontinuity or moments of rupture we learn a great deal about the questionable claims of continuity and order. For example, a period of fractious strikes in the early years of industrial capitalism might reveal a good deal about the supposedly harmonious and mutually beneficial social development under capitalism. A period of violent social protest might reveal a good deal about a country's supposedly tranquil political order. Proponents of antifoundationalism contend that discontinuity is an apt description of how social development actually occurs—as opposed to the structural-functionalist model of orderly evolution—as well as a convenient weather vane for social order and dissent.

Three implications follow from this idea of discontinuity. First, the rationale for linear explanations is called into question. Linear explanations are a prerequisite for any attempt to construct cause-and-effect arguments. This is done by placing a particular event within a larger sequence of logically arranged events. An individual event is, on the one hand, explained by the larger sequence and, on the other hand, it allows the larger sequence of events to realize its destiny. Consider the underground railroad. In one sense, the underground railroad was an event within a larger linear process— the abolitionist movement in the United States. Thus, the underground railroad can be said to fit within a larger pattern of events that made up the abolitionist movement. At the same time, it was a key development that helped the abolitionist movement realize its goal of emancipation. Proponents of antifoundationalism argue that such a portrayal does not allow one to understand the underground railroad on its own merits and outside the perspective of the abolitionist movement.

Second, there is a flat rejection of any type of evolutionary (or stagist), mechanical model of social development. An evolutionary model of social development involves a model made up of sequential stages that a society is expected to pass through. A society's level of progress is based on which stage it has achieved. Such an approach, proponents of antifoundationalism argue, leads the observer to inevitably characterize a society on the basis of the model and not on the actual, individual case. If the evolutionary process is a given, then one needs only to be concerned with a small set of common factors (population growth, literacy rates, cost of living, etc.) that can be measured across all societies. Just as in the case of the underground railroad, the unique circumstances of a particular case are irrelevant. The role of the model is not to help us better understand the case. The case helps us to better understand the model.

Third, there are no regular, predictable patterns that mark the course of human events. Consistent with this, antifoundationalism rejects the search for universal laws that conveniently explain social developments in broad generalizations. Regular patterns and universal laws presume a degree of stability and permanence across society that does not exist. What today appears to be a new stage of universal history (the dot-com frenzy of the 1990s) may seem at a later point (following the dot-com crash) to be misplaced exuberance. If the interpretation of an event is subject to such great swings of judgment over the course of time, then it is foolish to characterize events as exhibiting regular, predictable patterns. Proponents of antifoundationalism, therefore, favor the study of specific cases over general classifications and local interpretations over categorical explanations.

FURTHER READING

Ashley, David. "Postmodernism and Antifoundationalism." Pp. 53–75 in *Postmodernism and Social Inquiry*. Edited by David Dickens and Andrea Fontana. New York: Guilford, 1994.

Best, Steven, and David Kellner. "In Search of the Postmodern." Pp. 1–34 in *Postmodern Theory: Critical Interrogations*. New York: Guilford, 1991.

Lyon, David. "Postmodernity: The History of an Idea." Pp. 4–18 in *Postmodernity: Concepts in Social Thought*. Minneapolis: University of Minnesota Press, 1994.

Rosenau, Pauline. "Into the Fray: Crisis, Continuity, and Diversity." Pp. 3–24 in *Post-Modernism and the Social Sciences*. Princeton, N.J.: Princeton University Press, 1991.

West, David. "Postmodernism." Pp. 189–220 in *An Introduction to Continental Philosophy*. Cambridge, UK: Polity Press, 1996.

7

Yes, But . . . Now What?

The foregoing chapters sketched the major issues and debates that have given rise to contemporary social research methods. Fueling this discussion has been the notion that the investigator plays an active role within social research, making a number of methodological choices that have far-reaching consequences for all aspects of his or her work. In particular, these choices determine the types of questions that can be asked and the forms of knowledge that can be generated. These choices are not always explicit or even well understood by the researcher. Importantly, the less explicit a researcher is with respect to methodological choices, the less aware he or she is of the fundamental limitations of his or her work. Ideally, one strives to conduct social research that is both informed and intentional. This requires researchers who (a) understand (and consciously wrestle with) the methodological choices available to them and who (b) interpret their findings within the limits of these choices.

The aim of this final chapter is to put these methodological choices in somewhat sharper relief. Previous chapters have sketched four distinct (yet overlapping) methodological orientations: postpositivism, structuralism, hermeneutics, and antifoundationalism. (Given that embryonic positivism and logical positivism have largely culminated in postpositivism, the focus here is on the latter.) In each case, certain contradictions or tensions within social research gave rise to new methodological approaches, which, in turn, fostered further unsettling inconsistencies. Such contradictions or inconsistencies represent dynamic tensions across social research that mark the fault lines separating the methodological orientations outlined in this book. Consequently, highlighting these tensions provides a deeper understanding of the unique perspectives and contributions that each approach offers.

In addition to reviewing the dynamic tensions associated with each methodological orientation, it is useful to consider their consequences in a specific scenario. Therefore, after discussing these tensions, we turn to the case of an undergraduate student who wishes to better understand race relations on campus. By detailing the implications of the student researcher's methodological choices in such a case, it will become clear how certain questions about race relations are permitted, for example, by postpositivism that are not permitted by antifoundationalism (and vice versa). At the same time, some forms of knowledge regarding race relations may be a central focus from a structuralist perspective but of only marginal interest for hermeneutics (and vice versa). By exploring these differences, both the role of the researcher as an active agent and the consequences of his or her choices are highlighted.

DYNAMIC TENSIONS WITHIN RESEARCH METHODS

As social research advances into the early twenty-first century, it is marked by certain dynamic tensions that both facilitate and complicate a researcher's world. These tensions help outline the basic limitations and opportunities associated with postpositivism, structuralism, hermeneutics, and antifoundationalism. As detailed in previous chapters, each of these methodological orientations first emerged from a growing disenchantment with some previous method of social investigation. Each then developed a unique set of methodological alternatives.

As a consequence, all of the surviving methodological orientations today share two basic characteristics. (1) Each stems from the desire to address some defect in a previous method. (2) In the course of its own development, each methodological orientation has been associated with a unique set of dynamic tensions. The basic difference between a defect and a dynamic tension is that, in the former case, it is argued that there are particular features of an approach that make it incapable of properly understanding the social world and it must be abandoned. In the latter case, it is recognized that there may be troubling ambiguities or contradictions within a methodological orientation, but researchers opt to live with this ambiguity for the sake of gaining certain, if imperfect, insight. (For a more detailed treatment of each dynamic tension discussed below, the reader is encouraged to review the appropriate chapter and turn to the suggested further reading.)

Tensions Raised by Postpositivism

There are six dynamic tensions raised by postpositivism. The first concerns the ideal of untainted observation versus the claim that all observations are inherently theory laden. A central premise of empiricism turns on the ability to make reliable observations of social phenomena. Today, postpositivists question the researcher's ability to make observations that are untainted by his or her approach to the subject. Because all observations are preceded by a number of theoretical and methodological assumptions that frame a research project, it is argued that all observations are in fact viewed through the prism of these assumptions. They are theory laden.

The second tension raised by postpositivism concerns universal claims versus relativistic judgments. A cornerstone of earlier interpretations of positivism was the goal of establishing universal claims that were applicable across different societies and settings. Postpositivists, by contrast, concern themselves with the limitations of applying statements across various societies and settings. Statements are often specific to a particular group with a common language game. For this reason, it is argued that to some degree judgments must be seen as relative to other judgments with reference to one's local language game.

The third tension raised by postpositivism concerns eternal truths versus the provisional (historically bound) nature of truth. Not only is the truth of a judgment specific to a particular language game, but, furthermore, it can only be said to be temporarily valid. A statement that is today judged true (same-sex marriage is incompatible with the dominant U.S. cultural values and beliefs) may not remain so as circumstances change. For this reason, all judgments are considered provisional.

The fourth tension raised by postpositivism concerns objective facts versus intersubjective agreement. Previous generations of positivists had sought to construct a reliable procedure by which an individual could observe the world and render true, objective facts. When this proved problematic—there was no way to consistently evaluate the accuracy of two persons' contradictory observations of the same phenomenon—the standard of intersubjective agreement was promoted. A community of observers (such as a panel of trained scientists) replaced the lone researcher. For this reason, the standard of replicability is highly valued by postpositivist researchers.

The fifth tension raised by postpositivism concerns a single standard of reason versus the reliance on multiple patterns of reasoning. Early positivists were convinced that the physical sciences relied upon a single standard of reason and that this could be adopted by the social sciences. Today, postpositivists believe that social research must rely on multiple patterns of reasoning that are combined to produce a version as close to the truth as possible. This position is somewhat at variance with those who suggest that language games prevent a unified understanding. In this case, the use of multiple patterns of reasoning attempts to combine judgments from different settings (or language games) to expand the researcher's understanding.

The sixth tension raised by postpositivism concerns linear versus nonlinear progress. Postpositivists are in general agreement that the study of social progress is the purpose of social research. There is less agreement, however, concerning the nature of this progress. Some maintain that social progress is a linear process of development that can be observed and measured. Others believe that social progress is at times nonlinear. Innovations and discoveries often break so thoroughly from a previous era's beliefs and assumptions as to defy any direct, linear rationale.

Tensions Raised by Structuralism

There are five dynamic tensions raised by structuralism. The first concerns the emphasis on (concrete) parts versus (abstract) wholes. The distinction between parts and wholes is long-standing. Akin to inductive reasoning, much social research begins with the observation and measurement of parts to better understand the whole. Structuralists emphasize the analysis of the whole (the global economy) to better understand the parts (a single nation's economy). In this sense, parts play specific roles within wholes that can only be understood by examining the whole itself.

The second tension raised by structuralism concerns individual autonomy versus structural determinacy. This distinction follows from that of parts and wholes. Those who focus on parts emphasize individual autonomy—a nation's right to establish its own labor laws. By contrast, those who focus on wholes emphasize structural determinacy—the pressures of the global economy on nations to weaken their labor laws. Striking the right balance between these two extremes can be a significant challenge in social research.

The third tension raised by structuralism concerns the primacy of empiricism versus the primacy of rationalism. Within social research, empiricism involves the observation and measurement of parts. Rationalism involves the analysis of wholes through generalizations and laws. Given the structuralists' emphasis on wholes, there is a tendency to value rationalism over empiricism.

The fourth tension raised by structuralism concerns drawing no distinctions between the unit of analysis and the unit of observation versus drawing such distinctions. For those who emphasize parts over wholes, there is little distinction between the unit of analysis (a mob that represents a unique combination of discrete parts) and the unit of observation (the distinguishable individuals who make up a mob). For those who emphasize wholes over parts, there is a significant distinction between the unit of analysis (the social conditions giving rise to a mob) and the unit of observation (the mob as a social mass, whose members do not represent discrete parts).

The fifth tension raised by structuralism concerns historical versus ahistorical explanations. One of the major dividing points for structuralists concerns this distinction between a static versus a dynamic analysis. Some argue that there are universal and unchanging, prewired structures that shape language and social organization across all societies. Others argue that the structures that organize society are evolving, historical entities that take different forms in different times and places.

Tensions Raised by Hermeneutics

There are six dynamic tensions raised by hermeneutics. The first concerns explanation versus understanding as the goal of research.

Hermeneutic researchers contend that the purpose of social research is to improve our understanding of society. This contrasts with the positivists' emphasis on explanation. It is hoped that understanding will help to develop a deeper, more nuanced portrait of certain social phenomena. With explanation, the goal is to identify causal mechanisms that explain social phenomena.

The second tension raised by hermeneutics concerns nomothetic versus idiographic social research. Nomothetic social research emphasizes generalizations (covering laws) that explain social phenomena. Idiographic social research emphasizes the development of detailed, descriptive accounts of social phenomena. Hermeneutic research relies heavily on idiographic research, which can take the form of intensive case studies that do not result in broad generalizations (or covering laws).

The third tension raised by hermeneutics concerns objectivity versus subjective interpretation. The aim of positivist social research is to create as objective an account of social phenomena as possible and to minimize subjective bias. By contrast, hermeneutics highlights subjectivity. The role of subjective bias as a factor in social organization is a central focus that guides hermeneutic research.

The fourth tension raised by hermeneutics concerns observation and measurement versus interpretation (*verstehen*) as the core activity of social research. Those who emphasize observation and measurement assume that the social world is somehow accessible through empirical techniques. Within hermeneutics, by contrast, it is contended that all such attempts to describe the social world are in fact merely interpretations of the social world. For this reason, proponents of hermeneutics focus on how competing interpretations of social phenomena are constructed.

The fifth tension raised by hermeneutics concerns selecting a single (most accurate) explanation versus identifying a plurality of meanings. Many postpositivists remain committed to social research aimed at identifying the single best explanation of social phenomena—based on cultivating a free and open debate among researchers. Hermeneutic researchers argue that social reality is such that, for any given social phenomenon, there are multiple meanings. Because there are no universal criteria, no one interpretation can be definitively judged superior to another.

The sixth tension raised by hermeneutics concerns an author's original meaning versus a historical interpretation of a text. Within hermeneutics there has always been a debate regarding the proper approach to interpreting a text. On the one hand, there are those who strive for the literal reading of a text (based on reconstructing the original author's true meaning). On the other hand, there are those who believe that because all texts are the products of broader historical circumstances they must be interpreted, not by strictly reconstructing the original author's intent, but on the basis of the historical circumstances that defined the author's social world. In this way, some Christian sects believe that the words of their Messiah must be taken literally while others place these words in their historical and cultural context.

Tensions Raised by Antifoundationalism

There are five dynamic tensions raised by antifoundationalism. The first concerns models that reflect reality as it truly is versus explanations based on metaphors. There are many critiques of efforts to create models that reflect reality as it truly is. Antifoundationalists argue that these models represent metaphors for how one sees the world. In this way, the models reveal more about how someone attributes meaning to social phenomena than about the actual social world.

The second tension raised by antifoundationalism concerns the supposed neutrality of knowledge versus the inherent link between knowledge and power. Antifoundationalists reject the notion that knowledge represents a set of objective truths that people then use for good or evil. Rather, they view the development of knowledge itself as a reflection of underlying social power relations. In other words, what is promoted as the most advanced knowledge is determined by persons in power in an effort to preserve their own privileged position.

The third tension raised by antifoundationalism concerns linear, cumulative progress versus discontinuity and rupture. With respect to social development, antifoundationalists emphasize those moments and events that break from linear, evolutionary progress. It is argued that linear, cumulative progress is an artificial construct that is imposed on a chaotic social order to satisfy some theorists' preconceived notions of social development. It is a pure distortion.

The fourth tension raised by antifoundationalism concerns knowledge claims as universal findings versus knowledge claims as narratives. Antifoundationalists reject the possibility of universally valid knowledge claims about the social world. Rather, a knowledge claim is treated as a type of narrative. Narratives are ideological frameworks that legitimize certain social institutions and practices by setting the criteria for judgments. (This is similar to Wittgenstein's language games.) Given this interpretation, no knowledge claim can be considered universal.

The fifth tension raised by antifoundationalism concerns generalizations versus individual case studies. At the core of much social research is the goal of constructing generalizations and laws that try to explain social phenomena. By contrast, antifoundationalists contend that the proper goal of social research is to construct intensive case studies. (This is similar to much hermeneutics research.) An intensive case study creates a detailed description of a given social phenomenon that can lead to a deeper understanding or new interpretation of that phenomenon that breaks with established tradition. Case studies do not result in generalizations or laws—though their findings may contradict and overturn existing generalizations or laws.

UNDERSTANDING RACIAL TENSION ON A COLLEGE CAMPUS

As suggested above, when it comes to conducting social research, as researchers we are all implicated. That is to say, the topic one selects, the manner in which one frames a question, and one's specific method of investigation all are choices on the part of the researcher—conscious or otherwise. For a deeper appreciation of the researcher's active role and the consequences of his or her decisions when conducting social research, it is helpful to consider a specific case. Each semester, great masses of social science majors are herded through introductory research methods courses across the United States. A common task for these students is to carry out some kind of social research project.

Given that race relations can be a hot topic on college campuses, students often select this as their research subject. In particular, students want to better understand the issue of racial tension on their college campus. For research to commence, our student must first select a method of investigation. As will be seen, this first step greatly shapes the study's final outcome. By comparing and contrasting the implications of competing methodological approaches for such a study, it is hoped that the role of the undergraduate student researcher will be further clarified. In particular, we will focus on the implications of the researcher's choices in two areas: (a) framing the research question and (b) selecting techniques of investigation.

Framing the Research Question

By now it should be clear that each methodological orientation approaches the same subject matter from a unique vantage point. Differences in this regard are reflected in how a research question is framed. Having selected a topic—racial tension on campus—our student must decide upon a method of investigation. Based on our review of social research methods, we can present her with four options: postpositivism, structuralism, hermeneutics, and antifoundationalism. For each, a distinct set of research questions follows. (Note that the sample questions do not by any means exhaust the range of possible questions from each perspective.)

From the perspective of postpositivism, the research question might be: *To what extent do students on campus view racial tension as a problem?* The basic assumption here is that racial tension is a real social phenomenon that can be observed and measured. The question further assumes that student attitudes are a good indicator of racial tension on campus. Student views regarding race relations are taken to be strong evidence of the state of racial tension. The primary challenge is to develop an investigative tool that will reveal racial attitudes among students on campus.

From the perspective of structuralism, the research question might be: *What are the primary factors shaping racial tension on campus?* The focus of research here shifts from student attitudes to a broader range of factors contributing to race relations on campus. It is assumed that to know whether racial tension is or is not an issue requires an understanding of the forces on campus that shape race relations. A structural approach attempts to analyze the forces that give rise to racial tension (such as a school's enrollment policy) rather than the manifestations of racial tension itself (a student protest).

From the perspective of hermeneutics, the research question might be: *What are the meanings that members of the campus community attach to "race" and what are the consequences of these interpretations for racial tension?* The assumption here is that racial tension, to the extent it exists on campus, is only understandable in the context of the meanings that people attribute to the concept of race. By understanding how different members of the campus community view race (divisive, harmonious, unimportant, etc.), the researcher will be able to patch together a variety of perspectives on race relations that constitute the context for racial tension. These perspectives may contribute to (or temper) racial tension on campus.

From the perspective of antifoundationalism, the research question might be: *What forms of social power are legitimizing our understanding of racial tension on campus and how do these reflect and reinforce the dominant racial order?* In this case, racial tension is inseparable from an underlying labyrinth of power relations that define a college campus. Racial tension, as such, has many narratives. The narrative of racial tension among members of the Black Students Union, for instance, is likely to differ from that among the clerical support staff. The researcher wants to know how different campus constituencies frame the concept of racial tension in a manner that (a) reflects their own power position and that (b) reinforces the norms of the dominant racial order on campus.

Selecting Techniques of Investigation

Once a research question is settled on, the actual research project can involve a number of investigative techniques. For example, our student might conduct interviews, develop a survey, review campus documents and records (e.g., college handbooks, campus security records), or opt for direct observation of campus life. In each instance, as in the case of framing the research question, the way each technique is used and the type of data collected will vary according to the student's methodological orientation. Let's suppose that our student has opted to carry out a content analysis of the college newspaper to investigate racial tension on campus.

In the case of postpositivist research, the purpose of analyzing the newspaper will be to find evidence of racial tension as captured in its news coverage. Content analysis will focus on those articles that provide a direct measure of racial tension on campus, such as a story on a racial incident and related editorials and letters to the editor. The researcher will use these items as a measure of racial tension on campus. Both the facts of the cases and the attitudes expressed by the campus community about the facts will be of interest. The selection of articles will be determined by their relevance to an actual case of racial conflict on campus. On the basis of these articles, the researcher will be able to make certain judgments regarding the severity of racial tension on campus.

In the case of structuralism, the purpose of analyzing the newspaper will be to detail how the newspaper, through its news coverage, contributes to racial tension on campus. Content analysis will focus on how articles are written in a manner that downplays, inflames, or ignores racial tension. The details of the specific cases of racial conflict covered by the newspaper are not of primary interest. The focus is on the role of the newspaper's coverage as a factor in racial tension. Does the newspaper's coverage lead to further conflict, to pacification and neglect, or to an open campus debate? The selection of articles will focus primarily on those that depict instances of overt racial conflict and their aftermath. (For this reason, for a structuralist to choose the strategy of analyzing the newspaper presumes knowledge on the part of the researcher that there has been prior racial tension on campus. This is true for the postpositivist researcher as well.) Campus events following the newspaper's coverage of an incident of racial conflict will be a major focus. Editorials and letters to the editor will also be of strong interest.

In the case of hermeneutics, the purpose of analyzing the newspaper will be to interpret the meaning that its writers' attach to racial tension and to trace how this is reflected in news coverage. Content analysis will focus on how articles interpret the concept of racial tension and to what extent this reflects an underlying belief system about racial tension among the writers. The selection of articles will include all those articles that, in the judgment of the researcher, have implications for understanding race. Some articles may be of direct, overt interest, such as an article on a racial conflict. The relevance of others may be less obvious, such as an article on changes in the dining halls in which the reporter neglects to provide comments from representatives of multicultural student groups.

In the case of antifoundationalism, the purpose of analyzing the newspaper will be to identify certain elements of a narrative that point to how its news coverage reinforces and legitimizes the newspaper's role as an arbitrator of (and authority on) racial tension on campus. Content analysis will focus on how articles adopt a tone and style suggesting objectivity and neutrality and how this both distorts the actual news items in question and conceals the role of the newspaper as an active, engaged agent regarding racial tension on campus. The selection of articles will focus on those that explicitly address racial issues. Of interest will be how the writers position themselves vis-à-vis the subject (as disinterested third parties) through the use of neutral language and an authoritative tone.

LOOSE ENDS

In the end, our review of social research methods has not resulted in any grand synthesis. While some of the methodological orientations discussed here do share certain characteristics, these approaches are primarily defined by their fundamental differences. For this reason, the world of social research can appear quite messy and unkempt. There seem to be many loose ends without a tidy resolution. As a result, all that lies before us is a clutter of choices. This book has attempted to clarify the consequences of those choices. Ultimately, it is the subjective judgment of the researcher (his or her choices)—and not a set of truth tables or decision trees—that drives the social research process. Consequently, it is sometimes necessary to simply leave loose ends loose.

Index

About the Author

David Baronov is an associate professor of sociology at St. John Fisher College in Rochester, New York. His previous publications include *The Abolition of Slavery in Brazil* (Greenwood, 2000) and, with Erik Pérez Velasco, *Bibliografia Sobre el Movimiento Obrero de Puerto Rico 1873–1996* (CILDES, 1996). He currently chairs a national advisory panel for the Behavioral and Social Science Volunteers Program, a national network of social scientists sponsored by the Centers for Disease Control and Prevention, and is pursuing research that explores methodological issues within community-based research.